Louis Honoré Fréchette

Christmas in French Canada

Louis Honoré Fréchette

Christmas in French Canada

ISBN/EAN: 9783741193682

Manufactured in Europe, USA, Canada, Australia, Japa

Cover: Foto ©Andreas Hilbeck / pixelio.de

Manufactured and distributed by brebook publishing software (www.brebook.com)

Louis Honoré Fréchette

Christmas in French Canada

Entered according to Act of Parliament of Canada, in the year one thousand eight hundred and ninety-nine, by GEORGE N. MORANG & COMPANY, LIMITED, in the Office of the Minister of Agriculture.

To
My Three Excellent Friends and Brother Poets
GEORGE MURRAY
WILLIAM MCLENNAN AND
WILLIAM HENRY DRUMMOND
THIS FIRST ENGLISH BOOK OF MINE IS CORDIALLY
AND THANKFULLY DEDICATED

L. F.

PREFACE

A MERE glance at most of the stories which compose this collection will convince anyone that the author is not an English writer. It may be added, moreover, that he entertains no ambition of ever becoming one. In his opinion, it is a sufficiently difficult task to learn how to master one's own mother tongue.

Then, why publish this book which is unavoidably defective, at least as regards phraseology and style?

In writing it, I had two objects in view. The first was to find a new mode of recreation, and the other, to do something to popularize, among exclusive English readers, this portion of the American soil called French Canada, with the characteristic features that she borrows from her *sui generis* climate, and especially from her people, whose language,

Christmas in French Canada

manners, customs, traditions, and popular beliefs bear an exceptional stamp, and must thereby be invested with a peculiar interest in the eyes of the surrounding populations.

To attain this last object, I have tried, in a few pen sketches, to convey some idea of the wild rigor of our winters, by putting, in turn, face to face with them, our valiant pioneers of the forest, our bold adventurers of the North-West, and our sturdy tamers of the floes, whose exploits of the past are gradually being forgotten in the presence of invading progress. I have endeavored to evoke some of the old legends, to bring back to life some picturesque types of yore, whose idiom, habits, costumes, and superstitious practices have long ago disappeared, or are disappearing rapidly. In the meanwhile, I took pleasure in leading the reader to some of our country abodes, into the settler's isolated cottage, into the well-to-do farmer's residence, beyond the threshold of our villagers, inheritors of their forefathers' cordial joviality. I have also invited the stranger into some of our city homes, initiating him into our family

Preface

life, into our intimate joys and sorrows, and introducing him occasionally to some old and pious guardian of our dear national traditions. This I have done with no other concern than to strike the right key, to place the groups in their natural light, and to draw each portrait faithfully.

Are these pictures in any way interesting? I can claim for them at least one merit: that of being true.

But why should I have penned these sketches in more or less awkward English, when it was so simple to write them in French, and so easy to secure a good translation from some experienced critic, familiar with the beauties and literary resources of the English language? The reason is no mystery: a translation would not have been my own work, and I would have missed my first aim, that of securing a few weeks of pleasant recreation.

I always read with renewed interest the French stanzas addressed by Longfellow to his friend, Professor Agassiz. The effort is apparent, no doubt; but there is a charm in

Christmas in French Canada

the effort itself. Surely, the recipient of this humoristic poem would have understood equally well some English effusion from the pen of the great poet; but nobody will believe that the satisfaction would have been the same on either side. As for Longfellow, he perhaps felt more enjoyment in accomplishing that *tour de force*, than in writing some of his world-renowned masterpieces.

After this honest acknowledgment, it only remains for me to tender my thanks to the distinguished artist, Mr. Frederick Simpson Coburn, who was good enough to seek inspiration in my little stories, and to take advantage of them to give the public, once more, proofs of the skilfulness of his pencil, and of his ability to interpret the different national Canadian types.

L. F.

CONTENTS

	PAGE
VOIX DE NOEL	1
ON THE THRESHOLD	5
SANTA CLAUS' VIOLIN	18
A GODSEND	34
IN A SNOW STORM	80
LITTLE PAULINE	98
THE CHRISTMAS LOG	113

Christmas in French Canada

	PAGE
JEANNETTE	129
THE PHANTOM HEAD	142
OUISE	169
THE HORSESHOE	184
TOM CARIBOO	202
TITANGE	223
THE LOUP-GAROU	241

ILLUSTRATIONS

PAGE.

"V'LA L' BON VENT! V'LA L' JOLI VENT!"
                                    Frontispiece.

"OUR DAYS PASSED IN CONTINUAL TRAVEL,"   - 10

"CLASPED THE INSENSIBLE WOOD,"   -   16

"WE WERE SOMEWHAT LATE IN ARRIVING AT ST. JOACHIM,"   -   -   84

Christmas in French Canada

	PAGE
"ALL PIERRE'S COUPLETS AND REFRAINS WERE GONE THROUGH,"	96
AUNT LUCY	100
PAULINE	103
"TO KISS YOUR BROW AND BLESS YOUR LITTLE GREAT HEART,"	112
CHRISTENING THE CHRISTMAS LOG	124
"DICTATED WORD FOR WORD BY HIS SPOILT PET,"	136
"IT WAS A HARD CALLING,"	144
OLD BARON	150
AT UNCLE VIEN'S	152
"I BRING YOU BACK A LITTLE SAINT,"	178
"AFTER WHICH IT WAS THE BEAR WE HAD TO DRAG TO THE CAMP,"	216
"TOM CARIBOO BEGAN TO DESCEND,"	221

Illustrations

	PAGE
"Looked like a Fritter out of the Frying Pan," - - - -	225
"Every Christmas Eve there is always a nice Dancing Hop," - -	228
"Beyond the Pointe-aux-Bapteinnes, God is Nowhere," - -	232
"Joachim Crete was Proprietor of a Mill,"	247
"Look here, Joachim, if you want a Place in my Berlot there is one for you," - -	252
"And He Fell on his Knees," -	258

VOIX DE NOËL.

Le lourd battant de fer bondit dans l'air sonore,
Et le bronze en rumeur ébranle ses essieux...
Volez, cloches ! grondez, clamez, tonnez encore !
Chantez paix sur la terre et gloire dans les cieux !

Sous les dômes ronflants des vastes basiliques,
L'orgue répand le flot de ses accords puissants,
Montez vers l'Eternel, beaux hymnes symboliques !
Montez avec l'amour, la prière et l'encens !

I

Christmas in French Canada

Enfants, le doux Jésus vous sourit dans ses langes;
A vos accents joyeux laissez prendre l'essor;
Lancez vos clairs noëls: là-haut les petits anges
Pour vous accompagner penchent leurs harpes d'or.

Blonds chérubins chantant à la lueur des cierges,
Voix d'airain, bruits sacré que le ciel même entend,
Sainte musique, au moins, gardez chastes et vierges,
Pour ceux qui ne croient plus, les légendes d'antan!

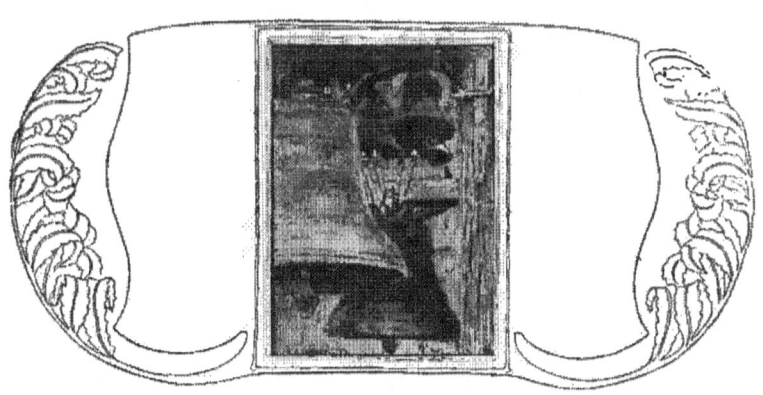

ON THE THRESHOLD

We were on our way from Montreal to Quebec, and during the evening the little group, gathered on the deck of the steamer, had fallen into a discussion chiefly on literary topics.

Of course some of us, (convinced or pretended pessimists), did not fail

Christmas in French Canada

to declare our modern progress, exemplified in trade, practical science, and industry, to be the inveterate enemy of all that was ideal. According to them, steam, electricity, and, above all, the spirit of Commercialism had killed Poetry: the Eiffel tower was her funeral monument.

"Pardon me," interrupted one of the little audience, whom the debate had attracted, in the easy fashion which rules amongst travellers, "pardon me, but you are simply uttering flat heresy. Poetry will never die so long as there is a heart beating in a man's breast. The ideal is within oneself, rather than in the world without. That which passes generally for the most commonplace object may, according to circumstances, assume a glorified aspect, or create an impression similar to that produced by lyrical or sentimental poetry of the most elevated description. All depends on the state of the mind, and above all on the point of view of the beholder.

"Take my experience, for instance: the most poetic thing I ever saw in my life, that which moved and stirred my soul with the

On the Threshold

most vivid and profound feeling, was an object so utterly commonplace that none of you, I am sure, would ever think of supposing it capable of evoking the slightest emotion. It was nothing more or less than a simple telegraph pole."

"A telegraph pole? Oh, come!"

"Seriously, gentlemen; I am not chaffing. Let me tell you my story, and you shall judge."

The speaker was a Canadian of French descent, strong and active, although well in the sixties, with an energetic face, a piercing eye, a well modulated voice, and the accent of a man of education.

We eagerly pressed him for his story, and without further preamble he began:

Gentlemen, I passed twenty-two years of what I may call my youth in a part of our country little known at that time, but which has been widely heard of since—the Klondike.

No one then dreamt of digging in that frozen soil for either nuggets or yellow sand. The sole industry in those regions was the fur trade. The wild treasures we sought were to be obtained neither by pick nor cradle, but by

Christmas in French Canada

traps and rifle, whether in our own hands or in those of the natives who frequented our trading posts.

I would not allude to the circumstances which led me there, were they not so suggestive as to the state of mind I was in when the incidents of my story took place. Here they are in a few words.

I was born at Rivière-Ouelle. My father died while I was yet at college, and my mother married a second time some two years later.

When I finished my course, my mother wished me to enter one of the professions, which would have suited me well enough; but this called for certain economies at home, which my step-father, with whom I had but little in common, determinedly opposed. Out of this arose discussion, misunderstanding and strife; in short, an impossible existence for either my mother or myself.

My poor mother! she had suffered from my presence; she was to weep over my absence.

Just because I loved her so tenderly, I could not endure the thought that I was a cause of distress to her. The only remedy was my

On the Threshold

immediate and permanent separation from her, and I took the first opportunity to apply it.

It presented itself in an offer from the Hudson's Bay Company to engage in their service. So I left home, and started for the North-West and the far off borders of Alaska, with a party of adventurous youths like myself.

I shall not dwell on my wanderings and the life I led at the different posts where I was stationed. Ah! I'll answer for it that any of those who think modern civilization too commonplace would have found there full opportunity to modify their opinion that primeval savagery is primeval poetry.

Of the necessities of life there was no lack; but those thousand and one little luxuries, those trifling refinements which make the charm of life, were not to be dreamt of. Of work there was plenty, and of the hardest, most exacting kind. But only at certain seasons. And how to spend the time during the rest of the year? Books were rare. What could we

Christmas in French Canada

invent to kill the awful monotony of the weary and interminable winter, face to face always with the same companions, and only able to mark the passing of the days by the short appearance of the sun above the horizon?

No news from home! Cut off from the outside world during twelve long months every year! Only one yearly mail, which arrived in the summer season, and that was all. Imagine twenty-two years of such an existence!

At length, during the autumn of 1876, the belated mail contained for me two pieces of news which brought me singularly closer to my old life and country. The one was that my step-father was dead, and that my poor mother, now old and infirm, was living only in the hope of my return. The other was that the newly constructed Canadian Pacific Railway had just reached Calgary, from thence to take a leap over the Rocky Mountains.

I was then at Fort Yukon, on the Yukon River, 300 miles to the northwest of Fort Reliance, now famous as Dawson City. I was free to leave. A Sioux, who knew the

On the Threshold

country and was returning to Edmonton, would serve as guide; with my heart throbbing with impatience I hastened my preparations for departure.

Thus it was that the morning of the first day of November saw me with my Indian, both of us on snow shoes, ascending the frozen Porcupine river, one man in front of, and the other following a long toboggan laden with provisions and baggage, drawn by four stout Esquimaux dogs. We were en route for Fort Lapierre, a good 250 miles to the East.

We would then cross the Rockies to reach Fort McPherson, seventy miles through a painful labyrinth of torrents, of precipices, of threatening rocks, of glaciers and towering peaks. For the poetry of savagery there was the scene. But I can assure you one was thankful to Providence when the poetic became less dominant and sank into comfortable and less dangerous prose.

Leaving Fort McPherson we had to follow Peel river for about 100 miles, when another hundred, of prairie, streams and portages, led us towards Fort Good Hope on the Mackenzie,

Christmas in French Canada

which we ascended to the Great Slave lake, a round of 600 miles this time.

From Great Slave lake our course was a straight line across the prairie to Athabaska Landing, our last station before reaching Edmonton—another march of at least 500

"*Our days passed in continual travel.*"

miles. No pleasure jaunt, that, nor a journey to be undertaken lightly, as you see. But even longer and harder stages may be faced with a light heart when loved ones await at the goal.

Our days passed in continual travel,

On the Threshold

interrupted only by halts for the mid-day meal. In the evening we camped wherever sufficient wood offered for our fire. When I say we camped, it is only a form of speech, for the camping was reduced to a very simple ceremony. First of all the dogs were unharnessed and served with their rations of frozen fish—for the dogs must be taken the greatest care of as they are the most precious possession on such a journey; after which, the fire being well lighted, we boiled our kettle.

Yes, we supped in open air, behind any kind of shelter, and oftentimes without any shelter at all, right in the wind and the snow drift. After supper, we had to dry our furs, damped by the exertions of the day; then we smoked, and at last stretched ourselves on the snow between a bear skin and a blanket made of netted hare fleece, with our guns close beside us—and *bonsoir, camarade!*

With the exception of our halts at the various forts and trading posts where we put, in a day of rest well earned and much needed we lodged thus every night *à la belle étoile*, up to the twenty-fourth of December when we had

Christmas in French Canada

counted on making Athabaska Landing early in the afternoon.

I had contrived a little bone calendar for myself in the shape of a horse-shoe, in which small pegs served to mark the date of the month and the day of the week. Thus I had kept track of time, and despite cold and fatigue, I felt cheered and comforted at the thought of passing the holy Christmas Eve— that feast dear above all others to the family —in company with those of my own kind, beneath a Christian roof.

Unfortunately, this fond desire of mine was not to be realized. Since early morning heavy snow had set in, driven by a strong north-east wind, which rendered our march slow and difficult. By noon we were in the centre of a bewildering storm, through which we could not see ten paces ahead.

Good Quebeckers imagine they know something of a winter storm. It would be cruel to send them to the confines of the North-West to find they have not, in reality, the slightest idea of what it is.

In those remote regions it is simply a thing

On the Threshold

of horror. It buffets and chokes, blinds and freezes one. Footing is lost, one stumbles at each step and cannot breathe; all sense of distance or direction is lost. Then nothing serves to guide; the sun itself shows only a feeble, diffused glimmer through the thickness of the air. Even the compass fails, and one staggers on at random, feeling the way, stiffened, panting, half drowned in the furious bursts and rage of the tempest.

Had I not been so bent on gaining the fort that day, we might have squatted down in some ravine, behind the shoulder of some protecting rise, under a bush—anywhere at all—where the storm might spend its fury over our heads; but I was obstinately determined not to camp in the open that Christmas Eve, and we went on stumbling ahead, even though our dogs would not stir without the lash across their backs.

But all our efforts were in vain; the fort seemed to retreat before us, and by evening it was clear we had missed our way. We were no longer in doubt of that when the snow ceased and the clouds broke sufficiently to let us see by the stars that we were wandering too far

Christmas in French Canada

towards the West. To reach the fort that night was an impossibility; there was no help for it.

Changing our direction, we struggled on for a few hours longer, not so much in the hope of making the fort, as of finding the wood necessary for our camp. I was literally broken with fatigue, and I followed the dogs, staggering with nerveless limbs, and with my heart numb with disappointment.

Suddenly the Indian, who was ahead, cried, "A tree!"

A tree! That a tree! Standing by itself in the open prairie? Impossible! The Indian must be dreaming.

Nevertheless, I slipped my axe from the toboggan and joined him. Sure enough, right in front of us, was a tall bare trunk without a single branch, standing upright in the open desert.

I stood for a moment in astonishment. But suddenly my heart leaped within me, and I gave a cry—a cry choked by a sob.

That bare, barkless trunk, that lifeless tree, emerging from the soil like a lonely mast in

On the Threshold

mid ocean, had been planted by man's hand. It was a telegraph pole!

We had passed Athabaska Landing and were on the trail to Edmonton.

Can you understand?

A telegraph pole! The advance sentinel of civilization. Was it not like a friendly hand stretched out towards me from the threshold of my own country? Was it not a greeting from a re-discovered world, the welcome to a living, cultivated land, peopled by intelligent beings, by comrades and by friends? Was it not . . was it not home?

I was re-entering social life after twenty-two long years of exile in the savage solitude. More than that, it was almost a re-entrance into family life, for that wire which I could hear humming above my head was a link between me and the past; it connected me with my village, with the paternal roof now dearer to me than ever, with my poor old mother, to whom I almost imagined I could send a cry of joy and comfort despite the weary 3,000 miles that still lay between us.

Can you understand?

Christmas in French Canada

Ah! but to realize what I mean, you must have felt it all as I did. Lost, as I was, under an arctic sky, in the midst of a frozen desert, with all the memories of the holy Christmas Eve in my despairing heart, my brain reeled before the unexpected symbol of intercourse, of fellowship, of civilization!

Before the staring eyes of my companion in misery, who, terrified by the weird song of the wire which vibrated in the sweeping wind, stammered "Manitou! Manitou!" I sprang forward with outstretched arms, clasped the insensible wood, fell on my knees, and burst into tears.

That is my story, gentlemen. We camped that night fireless and supperless, crouching round the pole; and through my dreams the voice of the wire boomed and rang, bearing to me, now the sacred hymns of the midnight service, now the carillon of the distant bells of La Rivière-Ouelle.

Take my word for it, I never attended such a poetic midnight mass in the whole of my life as that my fancy supplied in those hours of waiting and of hope.

"Clasped the insensible wood and burst into tears"

Page 16

On the Threshold

No, no, gentlemen, the spirit of Poetry never dies; it lives always in the innermost recesses of our souls, and the mere touch of those waves of realism, which, in the eyes of some people, threaten to drown it, is often sufficient to awaken its divinest thrills and to evoke its most heart-stirring melodies.

SANTA CLAUS' VIOLIN.

SUFFER me to introduce you to a quiet household. Although they were not exactly what may be called elderly, the father and the mother were no longer in their first youth, when, after one year of marriage, blessed by the Angel of happy loves, little Louis was born.

He was a charming baby, pink and white, with large black eyes, full of dreams. His mother rocked him almost incessantly in her

Santa Claus' Violin

arms, with tremors of wild joy, and his father watched his sleep at night, for hours together, awakened by hauntings of happiness and paternal pride.

The child grew up and developed under this double effusion of tenderness, just as some delicate plant unfolds beneath the warm influence of the sun, and the caress of the vernal breeze. He grew up full of grace and gayety, always fondled and always adored; no crease of a rose leaf had ever disturbed his sleep, nor had the lightest cloud overshadowed the soft brightness of his life's morning. He was decidedly charming; his smile seemed to radiate; the tone of his voice was like the warbling of a bird.

At the age of two, he made remarks of profound ingenuity. When he saw for the first time the silvery half-circle of the increasing moon, he called out as if in pain:—

"Quick, father! A hammer and nails; the moon is broken."

He was at the same time brave as a paladin.

Christmas in French Canada

"You must never go to the corner of the street," said his nurse to him one day.

"Why not?"

"Because there are savages there."

"Savages?" he exclaimed, with his fist on his hip, and a frown on his brow; "don't be afraid; I'll get my sword."

On the other hand he would sometimes lose himself for whole hours in strange reveries. One evening, there was great alarm in the house: the child had disappeared. Full of anxiety, they looked for him vainly right and left, in all the rooms, outside the house, everywhere. There was no trace of the little one.

It was late at night, and all were beginning to lose their heads, when some one discovered the child, alone on the balcony, with his chin in his two hands and his gaze lost in the open sky.

"What on earth are you doing there?" they asked."

"I am looking."

"At what?"

"Beautiful star."

Santa Claus' Violin

But that which characterized him above all was his passion for music: the sound of a flute called forth his enthusiasm; a flourish of trumpets made him start like an electric shock, and threw him into an ecstasy.

Let us add, by the way, that this sort of frenzy followed him even to the school-benches, where, at the age of eight or nine, the blast of a bugle or the roll of a drum made him irresistibly throw aside books and pencils and fling himself into the street without the slightest thought of asking leave, to follow the first detachment of soldiers that was passing.

But as it is with the baby alone that we are concerned, let us return to the baby.

If ever a child was passionately loved by his parents, it was Louis. But—the poor parents!—Heaven had a terrible ordeal in store for them.

The child was now fully three and a-half years old, and his mother discovered that a small tumor which for two years had been forming in his throat, in the region of the larynx, was developing in an alarming manner.

Christmas in French Canada

To use a technical expression, too pedantic perhaps, it was what is called in medical phraseology—a sebaceous cyst.

As is well known, those serous bodies are not generally attended with any real danger; but, in this case, the conditions were peculiarly critical, owing to the proximity of certain delicate vessels. The operation—which sooner or later would be necessary—might, if inconsiderately postponed, become dangerous.

The paternal devotion, after having deferred the cruel moment as long as possible, could not hesitate any further, and a few days before Christmas the surgeons were summoned.

With terrible anguish—need we say it?—the parents witnessed the dreadful preparations for what seemed to them the racking of the little being they cherished so dearly.

The mother, shut up in her room, wept every tear that could flow; while the father, in deep distress, and with bleeding heart, had to secure the poor little one on the sly in order to have him put under the influence of an anæsthetic.

Santa Claus' Violin

And in this way—yes, in full health and frolicsome gayety, with his eyes beaming, and ringing laughter on his lips—the dear baby's wrists were seized; and in spite of his struggles, he was made to inhale the loathsome drug, until he fell back, as senseless and pale as a corpse, on the table where the surgeon's knife was awaiting him.

Unfortunately, the operation was not so successful as could have been desired. At the most critical moment, the child was seized by a convulsive cough, and this accident, impossible to hinder, was followed by grave results. The cyst, instead of being completely removed, could only be partly extracted, and the wound had to be kept open for the secretion of what remained, by means of suppuration.

But we must abridge those painful details. The parents, who had sought refuge in an adjoining room, waited for the result in a state of mind more easily imagined than described.

"Well?" they both exclaimed at the same time, with the sweat of agony on their brows,

Christmas in French Canada

as they rushed towards the family physician who had superintended the operation. "Well?"

"It is all over," he replied gravely.

"Ah! and then...?"

"All is going well," he added, with an air and tone which rather belied his words.

"Ah! doctor, doctor, if there is any danger...!"

"No, there is no danger.... for the present at least. Only let the mother arm herself with courage, for unremitting attention will be necessary, and, perhaps, for a long time—provided no complications arise ...." he added with a shake of the head betraying his uneasiness. "At all events, fever has to be warded off by all possible means. The sick nurse has my written prescription. I will come back this evening."

In the evening the doctor came back.

He found the poor parents in utmost despondency: a high fever had declared itself.

During three long days and three long nights, the little martyr lay between life and death.

"If he could but sleep!..." said the

Santa Claus' Violin

doctor, who no longer took any trouble to conceal his anxiety; "if he could but sleep! . . . Sleep alone can save him; unfortunately, in his present state of weakness, it would be exceedingly imprudent to administer to him any narcotic. We must wait for everything from nature . . . . or Providence."

It was agony to the poor mother, confined to the bedside of her child. As for the father, he wandered distracted about the house, wringing his hands and longing to dash his head against the walls.

His son! his little darling! his idol! his only child! He accused himself of having killed him, and cursed his fate in a paroxysm of wild despair.

The child had had no sleep for over two days. He was insensible to all that was taking place around him, and the veiled glances of his large, glassy eyes, consumed by fever, wandered unconsciously through empty space.

"To-morrow is Christmas-Day, my darling," said the father, bending over the pillow wet with his tears, and covering with

Christmas in French Canada

passionate kisses the burning little hand which lay motionless on the bed, "to-morrow is Christmas-Day, and to-night Santa Claus will go his rounds distributing his presents among the little children who are lying asleep. Your new shoes are on the hearth-stone—there, just in the next room—you have only to say what playthings you wish to have, and if you sleep soundly, Santa Claus will bring them to you, sure enough. Sleep! will you not?"

And the poor father turned away his head to hide his tears and stifle his sobs.

"What do you want Santa Claus to bring you? Come, tell me, my treasure."

"A violin!" replied the child, with a gleam of joy in his gaze.

"A violin? Well, Santa Claus, I am sure, has some violins. Sleep well, then, and your good Angel will tell him to bring you a fine one."

But the child did not sleep; and the doctor, who came to see him several times a day was in despair.

"Ah! if he could but sleep! . . ." he kept

Santa Claus' Violin

saying. "If he could sleep, were it for one hour only."

During the evening, the child motioned to his father.

"What is it, my dearest?" said the latter, leaning over the bed to listen.

"Can he play the violin?" asked the child in a voice as feeble as a breath.

"Whom do you mean, my pet?"

"Santa Claus."

The father rose at once, tapping his forehead. A sudden inspiration, an inspiration from Heaven, had just passed through his heart and brain.

"Yes, my love!" he exclaimed, pressing the feverish hand of the child; "yes, my love! Santa Claus knows how to play the violin. He can play it charmingly, too; and if you will only sleep, there, on your little pillow, your Angel will have him play for you, and you shall listen to him in a dream. Oh! how fine that will be!"

And the poor father, with a last faint ray of hope in his soul, went out on tip-toe, while the mother, alone, knelt by the other side of

Christmas in French Canada

the bed, on which the little patient sat up, opening large, steady eyes in the dim light which glimmered through the transparency of the lamp-shade.

Night was coming on—the holy Christmas night.

The bells began to chime in the lofty towers in the distance.

But the child did not sleep.

The father, after an absence of about half an hour, came in again.

"I have just seen Santa Claus with his basket full of toys," he said, "and amongst them I have seen peeping out a jewel of a violin. He cannot fail to be here in a minute, for he was just coming out of a neighbouring house. Let us lower the lights; and you, my darling, do shut your eyes, and make, at least, a pretence to sleep."

He was interrupted by a slight noise that came from the drawing-room close by.

"Hush! it is he."

The noise became more distinct: it seemed as if some mysterious hand was secretly tuning the strings of a violin.

Santa Claus' Violin

The sick child gave a start, and listened eagerly. One might have heard his little heart beating in his breast.

Then followed a real enchantment.

Sounds of angelic purity floated through the silence of the night. Fragments of melodies of unsurpassed sweetness rippled in the air. Accents of infinite suavity, that seemed to emanate from the regions of dreams, spread themselves in wandering airs through the calm and restful shadows of the room.

The hand of the child trembled in that of his father, whose gaze, drowned in the twilight, watched with feverish interest the varied phases of surprise, joy and melting emotion which revealed themselves in turn, on the emaciated features of the little patient.

The latter kept listening.

For a moment the invisible bow seemed to obey some new inspiration. The capricious fancies of the prelude died away gradually, and little by little, veiled themselves beneath the texture of musical phrases, assuming a more definite character.

Christmas in French Canada

Melodies more clearly outlined began to pour forth in the sonorous vibrations of the instrument, and the ear could seize as it were on the wing a whole series, or rather an intertwined sequence, somewhat confused, but still perfectly perceptible, of those Christmas carols, so impressive in their antique simplicity—the work of unknown geniuses who knew so well how to blend the two poles of human life by causing at one and the same time, childhood to smile and old age to weep.

They all came out in turn, the good old canticles of long ago, solemn, but ever full of deep feeling:—"*Çà, bergers, assemblons-nous!*"—"*Nouvelle agréable!*"—"*Il est né le divin Enfant!*"—"*Dans cette étable.*" .. "*Les anges dans nos campagnes.*" .. And that "*Adeste fideles,*" so broad in its waving harmony, and so thrilling with Christian poetry.

All these melodies succeeded one another, fused in a marvelous whole, to which this nightly scene of speechless grief lent a character of intense and ineffable impressiveness. At length the child no longer

Santa Claus' Violin

moved, no longer trembled. The external world had faded away for him: he was literally entranced with ecstacy.

By degrees, the sounds becoming weaker and weaker simplified themselves into a sequel of modulations, lulling and sweet, through which the ear guessed—almost heard —the touching words of the popular carol:

> *Suspendant leur sainte harmonie,*
> *Les cieux étonnés se sont tus,*
> *Car la douce voix de Marie*
> *Chantait pour endormir Jésus.*

The father cast a glance on his child: two big tears were flowing down upon the little cheeks.

Then it was like the sighing of the breeze, like the murmuring of flocking humming birds, like the whisper of a stream amid the sedge.

Christmas in French Canada

With the softness of a caress, as it were, to the ear, the wondrous violin sang, or rather sighed forth the artless cradle-song which had so often sent the baby to sleep in the arms of his nurse:

>C'est la poulette grise
>Qu'a pondu dans l'église,
>Elle a fait un petit coco
>Pour bébé qui va faire dodo ;
>Dodiche! dodo! . . .

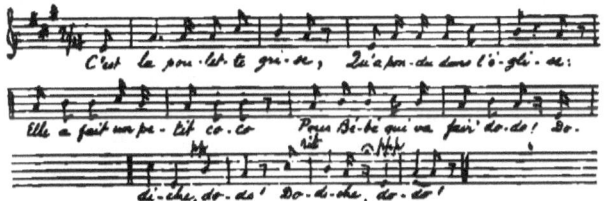

The little one shut his eyes, bowed his head, and his shoulder buried itself softly in the down of the pillow. Almost at the same moment, another head fell back on the side of the little bed. It was the poor mother, worn out by her vigils, who sank to sleep with a smile on her lips—a smile of infinite thankfulness to God.

The father, all perplexed with hope and

Santa Claus' Violin

fear, rose as noiselessly as a phantom and met the doctor at the half-opened door.

"He sleeps!" he murmured, quite beside himself; "he is saved, is he not?"

"They are both saved!" replied the physician, casting a glance into the sick chamber.

And in a rapture of gratitude the once despairing man burst in tears while he clasped the two hands of the great artist, Jehin-Prume, who had just replaced his violin in its case.

A Godsend.

IT is a modest hotel in Montreal.

With his back half turned to the window of his room, palette in one hand, and

A Godsend

brush in the other, a young painter is feverishly at work in front of a small camp easel.

On his left, pinned to the frame of a mirrored wardrobe, hangs an old canvas, about twenty inches by thirty, all dark and tattered, in the centre of which, through the besmoked tones of the clair-obscures, appear the graceful form and roseate complexion of an Infant Jesus resting on a cushion, the brow haloed by vague lights softly reflected from the glossy twining of fair and abundant curls.

From time to time the painter lets his right hand drop, and gazes at the picture with an intensity suggestive of profound admiration; and again he resumes his task, his brush passing between the mosaic of the palette and the canvas with an accuracy of movement which reveals the skilful and experienced artist.

He is evidently painting a copy of the beautiful Christ Child.

But why does he so often consult the modest silver watch, the old fashioned chain

Christmas in French Canada

of which hangs from his waistcoat pocket? This we shall soon know. Meanwhile, let us notice that his glance, with an expression of triumph, falls also, now and then, on some papers scattered on the small table beside him, and let us claim the privilege of the story-teller to ascertain what of interest those papers contain.

Here is, to begin with, a stained envelope, with broken seal, so rumpled, that it must have been opened many times. It must also have travelled a considerable distance, for it bears a Canadian stamp, and its address reads as follows:

Monsieur Maurice Flavigny,

Artiste-peintre,

Poste Restante,

Paris, France.

Let us open the letter and read:

Contrecoeur, *November 10th, 1872.*

My Dear Son,—A few words in haste to tell you how happy your last letter has made me by announcing to me your approaching return. Make haste, my dear child. Alas! I shall not be able to see you, but I

A Godsend

shall hear you, and I shall press you to my heart, as I did a long time ago.

I am still the guest of Mlle. d'Aubray, my little Suzanne whom I love as a daughter, and who is good enough to act as my secretary, since God has deprived me of my poor sight.

Come soon, will you not? Try and be with us by Christmas.

Your old mother, who longs to embrace you,

SOPHIE FLAVIGNY.

There is also a telegram:

NEW YORK, *December 22nd, 1872.*

TO MAURICE FLAVIGNY,
Great Western Hotel,
MONTREAL, CANADA.

If Murillo authentic and well preserved, will give ten thousand dollars. See agent Victor Muller, 4 Little Craig St.

CORNHILL & GRANGER.

Besides the telegram, bearing the same signature, but dated a day later, is a letter ordering a credit in favor of Maurice Flavigny, on the Bank of Montreal, for ten thousand dollars, payable to the order of Victor Muller, Agent of the firm of Cornhill & Granger, of New York.

Christmas in French Canada

This last letter the young artist has left open on the table, within reach of his eye, as if to convince himself at every turn that he is not the victim of a delusion.

Ten thousand dollars! A small fortune! He sees the paternal homestead redeemed; the good old mother saved from poverty; and, for himself, the necessaries of life, even an honorable and happy comfort, until reputation comes with its consequences in train.

He hardly can believe his own eyes. Does he dream?

II

And while blending his colors and hastily brushing the canvas, Maurice Flavigny reviews all the circumstances which have lately favored him in such an exceptional way, together with the events which preceded them.

He pictures himself, five years before this time, at the age of eighteen, bidding farewell to his family, and starting at random for the country of modern Art, in search of that science which develops talent, and without

A Godsend

which genius itself remains impotent and blind. He remembers his long days of feverish ambition, his weary nights devoted to ungrateful tasks, the buffeting he encountered, his disappointments, his moments of discouragement. He recalls the selfishness of his masters, the jealousies of his comrades, the humiliations he underwent, and all the pangs of his wounded pride. He lives over again his anguish, his doubt, his weariness, his home longing, oh! yes, his home longing, in the heart of that monstrous city where, by a cruel irony, all the pleasures seem to conspire together to invest one with the sense of utter solitude.

The first two years had been comparatively serene. Maurice Flavigny had been hard at work, striving conscientiously, living modestly on a small pension which came from his father—a country notary, proprietor of two small farms which yielded but a limited revenue—and spending his leisure hours in the museums, studying the great masters, and endeavoring to learn from their immortal masterpieces the secret of their inspiration.

Christmas in French Canada

He made rapid progress; and already glimmering hopes began to smile upon his ambition, when a series of casualties overthrew his fondest dreams and plunged him into distress and despondency.

Misfortunes impossible to foresee had assailed the paternal home. Unwise speculations had dragged the old notary to complete ruin. And on the very day upon which the house where Maurice was born was sold by judicial authority, his father died from grief and apoplexy, leaving to his heirs nothing but a life insurance policy barely sufficient to prevent his wife, who had lost her sight, from becoming an object of public charity.

She had been succoured by the young school-mistress of the neighborhood, the only survivor of an old seigneurial family, who had spontaneously offered her the hospitality of one of the four rooms which constituted her residence in the school-house.

All the details of these cruel events had been communicated to him by the young school-mistress herself, who had naturally to hold the pen for her to whom the saddest

A Godsend

of infirmities forbade all personal correspondence.

Deprived of the paternal pension, the young painter had been obliged to neglect his studies, and to give himself up almost exclusively to mercenary labor, in order to procure his daily bread. He became, like many others, the victim of heartless mercantilism, which, in Paris, as in other large cities, speculates on needy talent and draws the blood from the veins of poor young artists in exchange for a morsel of food.

During two long years he strove and lived miserably, without even succeeding, at the price of the most enslaving toil, in saving the sum necessary for his return home.

Then came the Franco-Prussian war, the seige of Paris and the horrors of the Commune.

The young Canadian, full of devotion and patriotism, had not hesitated; he had valiantly paid his debt of blood to the great Mother, and had been wounded at the storming of Buzenval, side by side with his master and friend, Henri Regneault, fallen also beneath the hail of German bullets.

Christmas in French Canada

Then the long months of hospital; and afterwards the harness resumed, the neck once more bent to the yoke to recommence the desperate task.

As he recalls these long years of distress, of hardship and sorrow, the young painter bows his head, and a heart-rending expression of woe pervades his features.

But suddenly his whole face radiates with a beam of joy. One of his paintings received and admired at the Exposition Salon; a rich amateur; a brilliant sale; his debts paid, and his return to America, with a future before him, at home, by the side of his old mother!

Unable to control his emotion, the young man paces up and down the floor of the room, and then stops in front of the table, gazes for a long time upon the bank draft —real, palpable, before him. After which he returns to his work, murmuring in a tone of supreme gratitude to God:

"And now, I am rich! . . Yes, rich! . . And this after my last resource had disappeared, with that unfortunate pocket-book

A Godsend

lost just as I set foot on my native land. Was the hand of Providence ever more visible?"

And the brush still hastens, fusing shadows, softening outlines and heightening the effects of light, till under the influence of feverish inspiration, a marvelous intensity of life flashes from the canvas, as the work advances, and the picture emerges radiantly from the rough draught.

III

But let us leave the artist at his work, and relate the story of this lost pocket book.

Upon reaching the Bonaventure station by the direct train from New York, Maurice Flavigny had ordered his luggage to be taken to a neighboring hotel, and had paid the porter out of the small change Europeans never fail to carry in their pockets for the exigencies of the *pourboire*.

But, after reaching his room, the poor fellow, with a feeling of despair one can easily imagine, found that his pocket-book,

Christmas in French Canada

which contained all the money he had in the world, was no longer in his possession.

All search was useless. Maurice was the victim of a pickpocket, and was left without even enough money to reach the village where he was impatiently expected by his mother, as poor as himself.

Maurice Flavigny yielded to the inevitable, wept silently, then fell on his knees and prayed.

The next morning some one knocked at his door.

"M. Flavigny?"

"That's my name."

"A parcel for you."

Much puzzled, the young man took the package and opened it. An exclamation of joy burst from his lips. There was his pocket-book together with a parcel the size of his arm, and a letter.

With his hand trembling with surprise, Maurice broke the seal, and read the following extraordinary epistle:

SIR,—The person who writes this is a stranger. Last night, he saw a pocket-book fall from your

A Godsend

pocket, and picked it up. If he returns it untouched, nothing is left for him but to starve. In consequence, he takes the liberty, in sending it back to you, to retain fifty dollars out of the hundred and ten which it contains. But, as he is not a thief, and has just learned, from the register of your hotel, that you are a painter, he leaves you in exchange an object which is useless to him in this country, but which, you can judge for yourself, is certainly worth the sum he has retained, and even more. He came from Quebec six weeks ago on foot; and finding himself endowed with very little disposition for that mode of travelling, will purchase a railroad ticket for Chicago with your money. God preserve you from the necessity of borrowing by such a process.

No signature.

Maurice Flavigny, at once relieved and perplexed, untied the parcel, and discovered the picture which we have just seen him copying.

He examined it rather indifferently at first, believing it to be like so many other pretended "masters," a perfectly worthless copy. But the more attention he gave it, the more he felt his interest awakened. It was something after all. No mistake, it was something! A genuine piece of old

Christmas in French Canada

art; a master's work; a masterpiece perhaps.

"What can it be?" he said with intense interest.

He spread open the canvas, took it near the window, surveyed it at a distance, then again more closely. Suddenly a flash of light passed through his mind:

"Can it be possible!" he cried . . . "An Infant-Jesus by Murillo! . . . Yes! this smoothness of tone, those aerial and waving shadows, those warm reflections of light, the moistness of the eyes and lips, the grace of the modelling, the morbidezza of the flesh, the harmony of the whole, both ideal and realistic, all the characteristics of the old Spanish master! . . . . . Every dash of the brush marks the signature. But here? By what miracle? . . . And, I am the owner of this treasure. Oh! my dear mother . . ."

And Maurice wiped his eyes full of tears. Passing through New York, he had made the acquaintance of wealthy dealers in paintings, who had said to him: "There must be some works of the old masters in Canada,

A Godsend

among the ancient French families. If you ever come across some of them the owner be willing to dispose of, please think of us."

"Holy Virgin!" cried he, "in three days from now, it will be Christmas; if I sell this picture I vow to paint a copy of it for the *crèche* of my village!"

IV

To paint the copy in two days was a hard task indeed, but it was accomplished. The original was delivered to the agent of Cornhill & Granger. The price agreed upon was paid, and with the copy he had made, neatly framed, Flavigny, the afternoon before Christmas Day, crossed the river at Longueuil, and there hired a conveyance to drive him down to Contrecoeur.

In the evening we find him knocking at the door of the presbytery, his votive offering in hand. The *Curé*, a good soul with some artistic tastes, delighted with the godsend, welcomed with extreme courtesy his parishioner, whom he knew by name only,

Christmas in French Canada

as he had been in the place but a short time.

He greatly admired the little *chef-d'œuvre* in which he found a kind of "familiar appearance," he said; and an hour later the new painting, adorned with flowers and evergreens, and suspended on the background of the sacred shrine of the parish church, above the traditional manger, awaited the midnight bell to radiate in the glow of lamps and wax-tapers.

Maurice Flavigny left the *presbytère* of Contrecoeur with an order for a large painting of the Holy Trinity, the patron of the parish. One can imagine what a hymn of gratitude rang in the heart of this youth of twenty-three, who, on this Christmas night, so joyful, so solemn, so impressive to all, was carrying both happiness and wealth to her he loved best in the world,—his old mother, poor and blind, whom he had not seen for five long years.

Maurice found her at the school-house, attended by only a young maid; the schoolmistress, who was at the same time the

A Godsend

organist of the parish, having had to spend the day in the vicinity of the church for the rehearsal of the Christmas music, at a cousin's of hers, a young physician recently settled in the village.

V

We shall not describe the meeting of the mother and son. Such happy scenes of overflowing tenderness cannot be depicted. The human heart is so constituted, that intensity of joy, like sorrow, naturally resolves itself in tears. Long did the reunited ones weep in each other's arms. And then—oh! the mysterious impulse of the soul which, in happiness as in distress, leads us to the feet of Him who is the source of all felicity as He is of all consolation!—the poor invalid took her son by the hand:

"Come, Maurice," said she, feeling her way as best she could towards a part of the bare wall, where her unseeing eyes seemed to contemplate some invisible object, "come, kneel down with me before the Infant-Jesus!"

Christmas in French Canada

"What Infant-Jesus?" asked the young artist, not noticing the significant beckoning of the little maid, busy with the dressing of the table.

"The Infant-Jesus of Suzanne, there, on the wall, the old painting she loves so well."

"I don't know what you mean," said Maurice, whose eyes, moving to and fro between the wall and his mother, still did not catch the glance of the little maid.

"Why! don't you see the picture on the wall?"

"Surely, no," said the young man, looking at his mother with anxious surprise.

"The Infant-Jesus is not there? . . . . The Infant-Jesus is gone! . . . Oh! pity on me! I dread to understand!"

And the poor blind woman sank on her chair, sobbing.

The little maid was questioned by Maurice, and after some hesitation, she explained all. During the last illness of Mme. Flavigny Ml^{le}. Suzanne, who had become entirely destitute, and knew not where to find money

A Godsend

for the medicines ordered by the doctor of a neighboring village—for there was no physician at Contrecoeur at that time—had sold the old painting to a stranger, a passer-by who had entered the house by chance. She had received a good price for it though, said the maid. Five dollars! Which did not prevent her eyes being red with tears when she parted with her treasure. She had warned the little maid not to say anything about the matter, especially to Mme. Flavigny, who, being blind, imagined all the time that the Infant-Jesus was in its usual place.

"Now," entreated the poor girl in conclusion, "don't tell Mlle. Suzanne I have betrayed her secret; she would not scold me, she is too kind for that; but it would grieve her. Would it not, Madame?"

Maurice's mother wept silently, while he, preyed upon by a strange preoccupation, reflected profoundly, pacing the room up and down, from one end to the other. After a moment he spoke:

"What kind of a painting was it?" he asked.

Christmas in French Canada

"Oh! merely old rubbish," answered his mother, "but the child had a love for it. It was a treasure to her. It was all she had inherited from her family—one of the oldest in Quebec; the last remnant of their former wealth, which she held from her grandmother, who left it to her, saying that it would bring her good luck. . . And imagine, the dear little one sacrificed it for me. . . Oh! Maurice, Maurice, what an angel! . . And so beautiful, they say! . . "

Maurice still reflected; at last he said:
"What size was the painting?"

"About three feet by two," answered the little maid.

"An Infant-Jesus?"

"Yes, with nice little golden locks, and lying on a silk pillow."

Maurice grew pale.

"On a dark ground?" asked he with quivering voice.

"Yes, sir, very dark!"

A Godsend

VI

For some time past, the tinkling of sleigh bells, mingled with the grinding of runners on the snow, hardened by the cold, had been heard at intervals. It was the parishioners hastening to church to prepare themselves for Communion, at the mysterious and poetic nocturnal mass.

Suddenly:

"Whoa! . . Whoa! . . Stop!"

Voices were heard at the door. One sleigh, two sleighs just halted.

"Who is it?" asked Mme. Flavigny.

"It is the Gendreau and the Benoit, Madame."

"Our old farmers, Maurice; you knew them; good people who do not forget me," she said with satisfaction.

"Walk in, *messieurs et dames*, walk in!"

"Good evening to all!" exclaimed the new comers.

"*Bonsoir, la compagnie!* How is your health, Madame Flavigny?"

Christmas in French Canada

"*Très bien!* It is you, Monsieur and Madame Gendreau? It is you, Julie? And your husband, I suppose?.."

"Marcel Benoit, *pour vous servir!*"

"Yes, Madame," intervened Gendreau, who was somewhat of an orator, having been a candidate for municipal honors, "here are Marcel Benoit and Philippe Gendreau, your old farmers, who never forget their good mistress, and who come with their wives, also present, to offer you their Christmas greetings, with all the compliments of the season, as big people say."

"Thank you, thank you, my good friends!"

"More than that, Mame Flavigny, we have just heard that your long expected son has returned home to-day, and as you are confined to your house, if you will allow it, we shall join here and have a good supper together after the midnight mass."

"You are too kind, indeed," said Maurice, who, absorbed as he was in his reflections, had remained aside. "Monsieur and Madame Gendreau, Monsieur and Madame Benoit, I am deeply touched with your thoughtfulness,"

A Godsend

he continued. "I know you have been excellent friends to my poor mother, and I am happy to have this opportunity of thanking you for it. As to the supper. . . "

"This is no great place for feasting," interrupted Mme. Flavigny.

"Tut! tut! . . you have nothing to say on the subject. We have brought all that is wanted. We know how it is when visitors are not expected."

"Come, Lisette! Come, Julie!" exclaimed Marcel Benoit, "show your stock of supplies. Here, look at this! Two hampers full: meat pies, tarts, a chine-piece of fresh pork, a turkey, and *croquignoles*,* real Christmas croquignoles, as we know you like them, Mame Flavigny."

"Yes, yes, yes! but we must not forget to mention something else," added Philippe Gendreau with a significant wink and strumming lightly on the round fat belly of a little stone jar; "here is some Jamaica of the good old time, Monsieur Maurice. The very thing your father used to like. I

---
* Doughnuts.

Christmas in French Canada

thought this would please you, and I hope it will suit your taste. Poor *Monsieur le notaire!* it is the remainder of a small keg he made me a present of on my wedding day."

Maurice Flavigny, moved to the heart by this simple friendliness, passed around from one group to the other, silently pressing the hands of each person, too much affected to otherwise express his gratitude.

"That's all right, then!" said Philippe Gendreau in his resounding voice.

"That's all right!" repeated Marcel Benoit, his faithful echo.

"*La* Louise will come," continued Gendreau, "to help the little *créature* to set the table. As for us, let us go. The last bell will ring soon. To church first, and the *réveillon* afterwards. Monsieur Maurice, there is a place for you in my cariole at the side of my wife. But, be careful, mind you, for she is somewhat ticklish."

Maurice, who was not a stranger to those jovial and familiar manners, heartily accepted the invitation, and after having put on his

A Godsend

heavy winter wraps, impressed a long and warm kiss on his mother's brow.

"*A bientôt*, my son!" she said; "go and thank the good Infant-Jesus for all the happiness he is bestowing upon us this evening. You will see Suzanne; tell her that she is expected here without fail after mass with her cousin, the new doctor, and his wife, if she is not afraid to venture out in the cold."

"Ho! ho!.. Get in, get in! Let us lose no time, *nos gens!*"

It was the thundering voice of Philippe Gendreau giving the signal for the start.

"All aboard! all aboard, *les créatures!*"

It was Marcel Benoit, who, according to his custom, seconded his comrade's motion.

VII

And gling!.. glang!.. diriding!

Here are the two joyful sleigh loads moving off at full speed over the creaking snow, under the stars glittering on their blue background like burning points of steel.

Christmas in French Canada

Gling, glang, glong!.. diriding, ding!

There they go, the fiery little Canadian horses, snorting in the mist, tossing their rimy manes, and exhibiting their well-known mettle,—Maurice Flavigny and the farmers' wives, warmly wrapped up in the depths of the carioles, while, standing in the front, well belted up in their wild-cat overcoats, with their fur caps pulled down to their eyes, icicles on their moustaches, and the reins passed around their necks, Philippe Gendreau and Marcel Benoit vigorously beat their bodies to warm their fingers, for the cold is fierce and bitter.

And gling!.. gling, diriding!..

Still they go, the brave little Canadian ponies, excited by more solemn and distant sounds which the wind brings to them in intermittent peals:

Dang! dong!..

It is the great bells this time. The big parish bells which sing their joyous carillon in the night from the lantern-shaped steeple of the old church of Contrecoeur, the tall windows of which appear in the distance, their

A Godsend

rosy gleam contrasting with the pale lights of the outside.

As Maurice Flavigny entered the church and walked towards Philippe Gendreau's pew, placed in the front of the Virgin's Chapel, face to face with the manger-shrine, a voice, sweet but powerful, a woman's voice full of emotion, accompanied by the strains of a harmonium artistically played, intoned the old carol often sung by our ancestors, that old hymn so touching in its ancient form and simplicity:

Çà, bergers, assemblons-nous !

Was it only the impression which every natural and sensitive heart feels at the sight, after long absence, of the old village church where he was baptized, where he received his first communion, and which echoed his infant prayers, or was it the effect produced on him by this silver-toned voice which he

Christmas in French Canada

heard for the first time? At all events, the young stranger knelt, or rather fell on his knees, hiding his face in his hands, his breast shaken by tumultuous sensations hitherto unknown to him.

When he raised his eyes, his copy of the Infant-Jesus was before him. From the midst of flowers, gold ornaments, and lamps of varied colors, the soft eyes looked upon him with an ineffable smile. Then, two big tears glided over his cheeks. He felt as though in a dream — and, lulled by the simple and impressive chants of this holy night full of sacred mystery, his thoughts involuntarily gathered in sweet memories and indefinite hopes which invaded his heart overflowing with emotion and happiness.

By degrees, the face of the divine bambino, which he did not cease to contemplate with the pride and interest of an artist, seemed transformed into the delicate features of a fair young girl with virginal brow, and eyes soft and caressing, in their supreme expression of kindness and sweet melancholy.

The whole scene also changed gradually.

A Godsend

Maurice saw this young girl, brought up in luxury, but condemned to work for a living, sharing her home with a poor, blind and helpless woman, and becoming her guardian angel, her daughter, her nurse. More than this, he saw her giving up for a trifle a family relic, a sacred keepsake, a masterpiece beloved and venerated, to save the poor invalid stranger. For he doubted no longer, the Infant-Jesus the copy of which had seemed familiar to the parish priest—that painting which had fallen into his hands by such an extraordinary hazard — that Murillo which had enriched him—could be nothing else but the old heirloom secretly sold to save his mother.

And this voice which so profoundly stirred all the fibres of his heart, was it not the voice of this young girl, of this modest benefactress—that of Suzanne? . . . And this name, half uttered, expired on his lips, like the most exquisite, but at the same time the most bewildering music.

Christmas in French Canada

VIII

The communion drew near. The voice which had just modulated the last notes of a touching pastoral became silent. A dying strain of harmony floated a moment in the sonorous depths of the arches. Then Maurice saw passing at his left hand, to approach the communion table, a fair, tall, young maiden, with an unusual air of distinction, modestly dressed in black, the sight of whom deeply moved him.

She knelt down, received the Sacrament, and then went and reverently prostrated herself before the Christmas shrine. But when she rose and lifted her eyes to make the sign of the Cross on her breast, she uttered a cry of surprise, and tottered.

With a bound Maurice was at her side, and supported her in his arms.

A few minutes later, they were at the doctor's house; but happily, Suzanne — for the reader has, no doubt, recognized the identity of the young girl—Suzanne did not

A Godsend

require his aid, the fresh outdoor air having completely restored her from the shock she had experienced at the sight of the painting.

When Maurice and Suzanne's cousin met, their surprise was manifested by two exclamations:

"Gustave!"

"Maurice!"

"By what chance, I wonder?"

"This is my home; and yourself? when did you return?"

"I arrived this very night."

"Is it possible? and what brings you here?"

"My mother. She lives with . . . Mlle. D'Aubray, if I am not mistaken?" said Maurice, bowing to the young lady.

"With Suzanne?"

"Yes, cousin," intervened the school-mistress, "the blind lady I spoke to you about is this gentleman's mother, it appears."

"What a coincidence! I have been requested to give her my professional attendance."

Christmas in French Canada

"In fact, you were an oculist, at Paris?" commented Maurice.

"Exactly."

"Ah! my dear friend, if you could ever . . . ."

"I understand; you may depend upon me. I will do my best."

"Thanks, but how is it . . ?"

"That an oculist should be at Contrecoeur instead of Montreal? Family interests, dear friend. The health of my wife demands country air—for I am married, my good fellow, married for the last six months. But I shall tell you all this on our way; I have just ordered my horse for the purpose of driving Suzanne home, and there is a place for you in the sleigh—with your permission, cousin?"

"Good! let us drive on, then!" interrupted Philippe Gendreau, who had just appeared on the threshold of the door, whip in hand, his faithful Achates at his heels.

"Let us drive on!" repeated Marcel Benoit, "the women are ready."

"You know we take the *réveillon* together,

A Godsend

doctor," added Philippe Gendreau; "it's understood."

"It's understood, doctor," re-echoed Marcel Benoit.

"Ah! well," said the doctor, "there is a *réveillon*, eh? That's another thing. You must wait a second, then. I shall have to do my share in it."

A moment later, the whole party drove away at full speed.

IX

On entering the school-house, the young mistress hastened to kiss Maurice's mother. It was a daily habit; but whether from the effect of one day's absence, or something else, the blind woman could not help noticing that "her little Suzanne" kissed her with unusual fondness that evening.

"Oh! such a beautiful midnight mass as we have had, Mame Flavigny!" exclaimed the farmers and their wives, Philippe Gendreau, Marcel Benoit, Lisette and Julie, surrounding the table burdened by a weight

Christmas in French Canada

of substantial and succulent country dishes, interspersed with lofty pyramids of *croquignoles* in their dress of powdered sugar—the traditional Christmas cake of French Canada.

And after a grace reverently pronounced by the blind lady for the blessing of that table around which sat all that were dear to her in this world, the feast began amidst laughter and joyful exclamations.

"Yes, a splendid midnight mass!" said the doctor. "Did you notice in what particularly good spirits the *Curé* seemed to be?"

"And what perfect singing!" timidly added Maurice.

Suzanne raised her eyes to his. The painter was seated by his mother; and the young girl had modestly taken a place at the side of her cousin at the other end of the table.

"Yes, yes, yes, that's all very well!" cried out Philippe Gendreau, "but in the meanwhile it's long time between drinks. Ladies and gentlemen, *sauf vot' respect*, Mame Flavigny, don't you think we ought

A Godsend

to drink a little toast between ourselves, were it only to have a short speech from Monsieur Maurice?"

"A capital idea!" emphasized Marcel Benoit, never too late when called upon to favor the views of his friend and candidate.

"Well, then," interposed the doctor, hastening to open a parcel he had left behind on entering the house, "if that be so, here is the moment for my surprise."

And he exhibited two sealed bottles, which—no matter what may be the opinion of the reader—did not seem too much out of place on the table of the humble schoolhouse of Contrecoeur.

"Champagne, upon my word!" exclaimed Maurice.

"Yes, champagne, and not bad champagne either," cried the doctor, with the nod of a connoisseur.

"A real banquet, then."

"Yes, the remainder of one tendered to me on the eve of my marriage, by my colleagues of the Faculty, my good fellow. It

Christmas in French Canada

is a joyous circumstance added to your happy home coming."

And the Doctor, after having popped the corks, filled the glasses and raised his own, saying :

"My friends, to the health of Madame Flavigny first, and then to that of my brave comrade, Maurice, who, by a happy coincidence, joins us on this Christmas night."

"Merry Christmas!" cried out all the guests, rising and touching their glasses across the table.

Meanwhile, Suzanne had disappeared.

The recipient of this cordial toast rose to his feet while the other guests resumed their seats. After having emptied his glass, Maurice opened his lips to utter a few words of thanks:

"My friends," he began—

But he stopped. A melodious voice, the same which had so much impressed the young artist on his entrance into the church, one of those voices which come from and go to the heart, a voice which conveyed by its freshness a peculiar serenity

A Godsend

of expression, sounded from the adjoining room, accompanied by the sweet and trembling notes of a melodeon.

The voice sang:

The last notes of the couplet raised a salvo of applause.

" Merry Christmas ! " cried the joyous company again and again.

Maurice kissed his weeping mother. Suzanne had resumed her seat at the table, and bowed blushingly under the gaze full of caressing emotion with which the son of Mme. Flavigny enveloped her. A current of mysterious affinities floated in the air. In a single moment two hearts held entrancing communion : most sacred compact which the Angel of Love signs in the face of God, with a smile on his lips.

Christmas in French Canada

X

Maurice tried to resume his speech:

"My friends," said he, "you have been drinking the healths of my mother and myself..."

He was interrupted once more:

"Wait a minute, here am I!" cried the joyous voice of a new comer.

A general outburst of surprise followed:

"*Monsieur le curé!*"

And every one rose with respect to greet the beloved and venerated pastor of the parish.

"Yes," said the priest, who held under his arm a somewhat voluminous object; "yes, Madame Flavigny; yes, Mademoiselle Suzanne, it is I, who asks your leave to share in your joy."

"Bravo! bravo, *Monsieur le curé!* Come and have a seat with us at the table."

"Certainly, my children; but first allow me to furnish my own share towards the general rejoicing."

A Godsend

Whereupon the good priest exhibited, to the admiration of all, the object he had under his arm, and which was nothing else but the copy of the Murillo so fondly painted by Maurice.

"My Infant-Jesus!" exclaimed Suzanne, bewildered. "My Infant-Jesus!.. Yes, it is He; it was not a dream... And quite new... Revived, radiant. . How can it be?"

"Mademoiselle," said the good priest, "I have just heard that there were for you some dear family remembrances and a touching tale of devotion attached to the original of this picture. You deserve that at least the copy should be yours, and I made it a duty to present it myself this Christmas night. The parish owes you more than this for all the services you render to our church from one year's end to the other."

"Merry Christmas!" cried again all the voices, while Suzanne, with folded hands, and still overcome with her surprise, said:

"*Monsieur le curé*, explain. It is not a dream... It is a miracle, is it not?"

Christmas in French Canada

"Yes, my child," answered the curé, "a miracle of artistic skill. Ask my new parishioner, Monsieur Maurice, who now must do his part towards concealing the theft I have committed to the prejudice of my cloth, and without the knowledge of my more virtuous church-wardens."

The young lady slowly turned towards Maurice and repaid to the young man the gaze with which he had caressed her a moment ago. After having divined, they understood each other. The sweetest emotion filled their two souls.

"Well, now, à *table!* à *table!*" cried Philippe Gendreau; "we are only beginning."

Another voice echoed:

"*A table!*"

Needless to ask if it was that of Marcel Benoit.

XI

"Monsieur Maurice, I congratulate you on your happy return," said the good priest, emptying the glass tendered to him by the

A Godsend

doctor; "God bless you in your ways, and keep you ever worthy of the pious mother he has favored you with."

"Thank you, *Monsieur le curé*, for your good wishes," said Maurice, speaking in a particularly serious tone; "I shall try to prove to you, this very moment, that I deserve them."

And leaving his seat, he passed around the table, and laid a large white envelope before the young school-mistress, saying:

"Mademoiselle, this envelope contains a bank draft for ten thousand dollars; it is a sum which I restore to its owner."

"Eh?"

"What?"

"How is that?"

"Ten thousand dollars!"

"What does this mean?"

"It means, my friends," answered Maurice, "that the original of the painting you have just admired, belonged to Mademoiselle; that it was the work of a great master; that it fell into my hands by chance, or rather by an interposition of Providence; that I sold it

Christmas in French Canada

for ten thousand dollars; and that I simply remit the price to whom it is due."

"But, sir," said Suzanne, whom so many emotions had rendered pale and trembling, "you do not owe me anything. The picture no longer belonged to me; I had sold it."

"Oh! no, Mademoiselle, you had not sold it. Like the good angel that you are, you had sacrificed that family relic which was so dear to you, in order to help my poor, sick and forsaken mother."

"No matter, Monsieur. Even supposing such a charitable action on my part, I cannot be considered as the owner of an object to which I have no claim whatever."

"Mademoiselle ."

"*Non, Monsieur*, I cannot take the money," said Suzanne, returning the envelope to the young man; "it is not mine."

"Then here, mother," said Maurice, placing the paper in the hands of the invalid; "give it to her yourself, since she will not accept anything from *me?*"

"Maurice, you are worthy of your father," said the good old woman.

A Godsend

And addressing Suzanne:

"My child," said she, "take this money, it is yours; it comes as the accomplishment of your grandmother's prediction; you remember, she said the old painting would bring you good luck. You have taken care of me, you have rescued me in my distress, you sat at my bed-side, you have saved my life; God rewards you for it by the hand of my son, and through the unconscious object which was the instrument of your charity. Take this money."

"No, Madame, it is useless to insist," said Suzanne, resolutely. "The money is not mine."

"But it is due to you."

"Madame Flavigny," said the girl, proudly, "even though I had some title to your gratitude it would be no reason for me to accept the price of a service rendered, would it?"

"And as for me, Mademoiselle," intervened Maurice, "I cannot keep the money which belongs to you. To enrich myself through your sacrifice when I am already so greatly indebted to your kindness would

Christmas in French Canada

be an act of meanness which would make me despicable in my own eyes. Do accept, I beseech you . . . Suzanne!"

He stopped, extremely confused at having dared to utter those two syllables which had so far ascended his heart only to expire on his lips. "Do accept," he insisted, "for your happiness and ours!"

"Impossible, Monsieur Maurice," answered the young lady hiding her face in her hands. "The money is yours; I shall never accept it . . . never! . . ."

Maurice let his arms fall helplessly by his side, and threw a glance around, as if to seek for advice. What was to be done?

"*Monsieur le curé*, speak!" besought the poor blind mother.

The two young people were standing facing each other, with downcast eyes, and in painful embarrassment, both perplexed and grieved in the contemplation of the unexpected wealth, fallen from heaven, but which neither of them could touch without a capitulation both of pride and conscience.

A Godsend

"Well, *monsieur le curé* . . . ?" said one of the by-standers.

"My good friends," said the priest, "the case is really a difficult one . . . Nevertheless, since God has sent this treasure, there ought to be some means of . . . The fact is that there is one means . . . but . . ."

"*Monsieur le curé*, I understand you," interrupted the doctor, joyously. "You have discovered the true and only means of making matters right. There is no other . . . And if, by chance, Mme. Flavigny had the least thought of asking from me the hand of my cousin for her son, after what I have seen at my house, on the road and here, I give her my word of honor that I would order the publication of the banns in less than two weeks."

"And it would not cost you much," cried the *Curé*, laughing.

"I'll take your word for it, *Monsieur l' abbé;* as for me, I have only one condition to insist upon: it is, that, in order to avoid all new conflict of interest, the future wife and husband be married

Christmas in French Canada

under the old régime: community of property."

"Bravo! Merry Christmas! merry Christmas!" ejaculated the delighted company.

Maurice and Suzanne were so confused that they did not dare to raise their eyes on each other.

The blind woman stretched her trembling arms towards Suzanne, who threw herself into them with a sob.

Lisette, Julie, *la* Louise and the little maid wiped their eyes with their aprons. Maurice bent one knee on the floor, took Suzanne's hand in his and impressed upon it a long and fervid kiss.

"Bless them, *Monsieur le curé!*" prayed the good old mother, also wiping her poor blind eyes. "Bless them, you, who can see them."

And while the old priest extended his long white hands over the two reclining brows, the doctor, who had stealthily and more than once observed the eyes of the invalid, drew near her, and whispered in her ear:

A Godsend

"You shall also see them in a few weeks, Madame Flavigny, take my word for it."

The little picture was bound to bring luck to everybody.

And if any one, at that moment, had passed along the road in front of the old school-house at Contrecoeur, he would no doubt have heard, mixed up with joyous laughter, voices young and old, clear and ringing, crying:

"*Noël! noël!* . . Merry Christmas!"

"We shall elect him a member of the council," cried out Philippe Gendreau.

"We'll elect him mayor!" exclaimed Marcel Benoit, who, for the first time, took upon himself to differ with his friend.

In a Snowstorm:

THE first time I stood godfather was under very extraordinary circumstances indeed, said the Judge.

It was well in the month of December, fully forty years ago, when for some reason

In a Snow Storm

or other, an election for the legislature was to take place in the county of Charlevoix, in January following.

Things happened in those days pretty much as they do now: all the young lawyers and other members of the professions who had aspirations for public life, were enlisted to assist; with their oratory, one or other of the candidates.

Living in Quebec at this time, and being one of the phalanx on our side, I was among the first called to the front. You all know what a task it is to carry on an election campaign in rural districts during the winter time; but, as you know, youth recoils from nothing when called upon to rally under the flag.

I had never visited that part of the country, which was said to be very picturesque; and, although the season was anything but favorable for a tourist, I made up my mind to undertake the journey, consoling myself with the thought that whatever the landscape might lose in peaceful beauty at this season of the year, would be more

Christmas in French Canada

than compensated for by its wild and impressive character.

My travelling companion was to be one of my class-mates of the Seminary, a promising young doctor, who, alas! was lost to science before he could give the world the full measure of his talents.

We both remembered that another classmate of ours had just been nominated *curé* of St. Tite des Câpes, and we got it into our heads that it would be a pleasant thing to surprise him by our presence at midnight mass in his new parish, where opportunities for worldly recreation were not frequent enough to afford him many occasions for indulgence.

A joyful evening *en famille*, between pipe and cork screw, and then an interesting midnight ceremony in some rustic chapel, after which a cheerful *réveillon* with wholesome *tourtières* and the traditional *croquignoles*, together with a few glasses of cordial to toast the health of our candidate, this constituted, you must admit, a simple but rather alluring prospect.

In a Snow Storm

Our plans were quickly arranged; and we started on our journey with a trustworthy carter by the name of Pierre Vadeboncoeur, who knew the road well, and a lively prancing tandem shaking their jingling collars in superb style and gait.

The sky was grey, but there was no particular indication of bad weather, and apparently nothing to prevent us from reaching our destination before six o'clock in the evening.

The box of our sleigh had been divided into two compartments; in the one we had placed our ammunition for the election, that is to say, the campaign literature to reinforce our oratorical flights; in the other all that we considered necessary to supplement the cellar and larder of our friend, who lived, of course, the simple abstemious life usual to our country *curés*, especially in those out-of-the-way regions.

I shall not give a description of the country through which we were obliged to pass; Beauport, Ange-Gardien, Château-Richer, Ste. Anne de Beaupré and St. Joachim are

Christmas in French Canada

all beautiful parishes; but from there to St. Tite, it is an interminable ascent across the most broken and desolate country one can possibly imagine; a dreadful road, plunging at times into dense forest, then winding up to bare summits, reached by rugged roadways creeping through fantastic gorges or sidling along dizzy precipices.

Such are the Câpes. This infernal tract is known as the road of La Miche. And the road of La Miche, that is the place above all the others where "the north wind doth blow," and where the storms of winter find full scope to unbridle their fury.

Now the weather, which had been reasonably fine during the early afternoon, had begun to change for the worse after our passage through the village of Ste. Anne. The snow—thick and dry—drifted from time to time by sudden gusts of wind, began to fill up the road, sadly impeding our progress. Consequently we were somewhat late in arriving at St. Joachim, where we halted at the house of an old fellow by the name of Filion, the keeper of a neat

"*We were somewhat late in arriving at St. Joachim*"

In a Snow Storm

country inn, to light our pipes and shake off the chill.

"*Messieurs*," said the innkeeper, "perhaps you will think it is none of my business, but if I were in your place I would go no further to-night."

"What do you mean?"

"I mean that Cape Tourmente does not bear his name for nothing; see if he has not the appearance of hiding himself for some mischief. Take my word, in half an hour from this, it will take no ordinary horses to cross the Câpes."

"Mine are not St. Joachim horses, you know," said the driver, somewhat piqued. "I have seen your Câpes before; I know what they are."

"Not so well as I do," returned the innkeeper; "and I wager you my house with all that's in it, that you won't go through the Câpes this evening."

"Well, well, we shall see," replied Pierre, lighting his pipe and tipping us a kind of malicious wink which we understood full well.

Christmas in French Canada

Filion—evidently an honest man—understood it also, for turning towards us he remarked :

" If these gentlemen suspect me of giving interested advice, I have nothing left but to wish them good luck; my duty is done."

We felt he was sincere; but to miss our Christmas Eve, our surprise for our friend the curé, was too much of a disappointment. And then Pierre Vadeboncoeur seemed so sure of his venture. . . .

In short, we re-entered the cariole, and while we warmly wrapped ourselves in the robes, the driver vigorously lashed his horses, who sprang forward, snorting, through the drifts.

The innkeeper had spoken truly ; in less than an hour, we were travelling blindly over impracticable roads, in complete darkness, enveloped in a torrent of snow and sleet, of which no one, who has not seen the same, can form an idea. After having mounted perpendicular escarpments, at the summit of which our horses could hardly stand against the wind, we had to descend into yawning

In a Snow Storm

gulfs, bordered by giant firs, where the poor animals almost disappeared in the whirling snow.

Of course, we could not advance at more than a walk; and with nothing but instinct to guide them, our beasts, exhausted and blinded by clinging rime, trudged painfully along with hanging heads and heaving flanks.

"Suppose we turn back," said I to the driver. "It is evident we cannot go much further."

"Turn back!" exclaimed the poor man, who seemed bitterly to regret his recent boasting; "it is too late, *monsieur;* I am as blind as my horses; in turning back, we would risk missing the track, and with the track missed, I would not give five cents for our three skins."

The doctor said nothing.

Our situation was becoming hopeless; since we could not retrace our steps, it was just as impossible to remain where we were, for the cold was increasing in a terrible manner, and in spite of our thick furs, we were chilled through and through. We had

Christmas in French Canada

no alternative but to advance—to advance at all hazards.

I was once in my life in distress at sea, with but little hopes of escape; but no agony of shipwreck can be compared to that which my companion and myself went through that evening, lost in the dark, solitude and tempest, half paralyzed with the wolfish cold, and depending on two wretched horses, which threatened at every moment to drop under the suffocating whirlwind.

This last calamity was at hand. Suddenly our shaft horse snorted wildly, and stopped dead, shivering with terror; the other one had missed his footing on the edge of a declivity, rolling on his flank, and struggling in his agony, half swallowed up in a flurry of moving snow.

"That cursed Filion has bewitched us!" cried our unhappy driver, throwing himself at the head of the second horse to prevent him from being dragged down by the frantic efforts of his companion; "if we have lost the road, there is nothing left for us to do, *messieurs*, but say our prayers."

In a Snow Storm

While uttering these desponding words, the poor devil had nevertheless succeeded in unharnessing the fallen horse. But what next? Leave the poor animal to perish in the snow? It was first to be seen if the other was able to continue the journey by himself. We got out of the sleigh, and rather plunged than walked to give help to the unfortunate driver, who, in spite of all, retained sufficient courage to endeavor to save his horses.

What a night, *mon Dieu!* I would not wish my mortal enemy to experience the shadow of the same.

Suddenly our coachman uttered a loud cry of joy:

"A gate! We are saved."

And so it was; on the other side of the road opposite to the slope on which the horse had sunk, our man had come upon a fence; and groping for a pole to help him in his work, he had put his hand upon a gate. A gate meant a house, and a house meant safety.

"Wait a bit!" cried the brave Pierre:

Christmas in French Canada

"in ten minutes there will be some one to help us."

And, in fact, to our great relief, he appeared a few moments afterwards with a man bearing a lantern and a rope. And, hurrah! There was our poor horse on his feet again.

"Good-bye now!" said the new comer with an extraordinary business-like air; "if the good God does not take care of you people this night, I pity you from my heart."

"What do you mean?" cried I; "do you think we are going further on such a road? Your house is near by; you would not leave travellers outside a night like this?"

"*Mes bons messieurs*," said the man with the lantern, "you are going to say it is not very Christian-like, but on my conscience and honor, there is no possibility of sleeping at my house this night."

"No possibility? But we are not exacting, *mon brave;* a little corner under your roof, two chairs, a bench, the bare floor—anything at all; but in the name of heaven, don't leave us lost in the snow, freezing

In a Snow Storm

alive in the depths of night, on this miserable road!"

"Alas! *mes chers messieurs*, it sounds hard indeed, but believe me, it is not my fault; it is impossible!"

For a moment he took our driver aside, but suddenly he uttered a cry:

"A doctor! There is a doctor here!"

And rushing back to us he exclaimed:

"The doctor! Where is the doctor?"

"Here!" answered my friend.

"Ah! sir," said the poor man, almost throwing himself upon the neck of my companion: "you are a doctor? It is the good God who has sent you. This way, this way, quick!"

By the light of the lantern Pierre and I followed with the horses.

"The stable is at the right," called out the man to us, dragging the doctor after him towards the house, the door of which he shut in our faces.

"I've an idea that there is no business for us inside there for the moment," said Pierre Vadeboncoeur, somewhat mysteriously; "but as my fingers are badly frozen, *sauf*

Christmas in French Canada

vot' respect, I think you had better let the others manage their own business and help me to unharness the horses."

"*Ma foi*," replied I, "one must adapt himself to the times; to help one another is a law of nature. Come on!"

And while the poor fellow, chilled through, and moaning with pain, busily chafed his fingers with snow, I drew our cariole under an open shed, and drove our exhausted horses into the stable. Then, after putting a bundle of hay in each of the mangers, I turned my steps towards the house, accompanied by Pierre, who was still suffering from the numbness of his fingers. He pushed open the door, and I entered, shaking the snow and frost which covered me from head to foot, and removing the icicles which hung on my hair and moustache.

Hardly had I entered, and in my haste to get near the huge stove which hummed away joyously in the middle of the room, let fall in a corner the heavy furs in which I was wrapped, when my *compagnon de voyage* appeared with a beaming face, carrying in

In a Snow Storm

both hands a small bundle, with all the precaution and reverence he would have displayed in bearing the Holy Sacrament itself.

"*Mon ami*," said he, bowing, "I have the honor of presenting to you a newly fledged citizen of the world, to whom I have just given, in the name of the Faculty of Medicine of Laval University, a passport for the stormy journey on the Road of Existence, without counting that of the Câpes."

"Is it possible—a new-born child?"

"*Oui, monsieur, pour vous servir*," said our rescuer, much disturbed but all smiles, "a little angel of the good God; our first!"

"On Christmas Eve, too! you might take him for the Infant Jesus Himself."

"It is indeed true; our little one is born on Christmas Eve!" cried the happy father, turning towards the open bedroom door.

"You see, then," said the doctor, "it is him, not me, that God has sent you, my friend."

"Him and you both, sir! all of you! you are all messengers of Heaven here," cried the brave man, drying his eyes with the back of his sleeve.

Christmas in French Canada

What then?

The baby was very weak, and considering the condition of the roads, it was absolutely out of the question to carry the little one to church for at least three days. Therefore, to calm the anxiety of the poor mother, so terribly unnerved by her trial on this night of storm, the doctor advised that a private baptism be proceeded with.

"You will not refuse to be godfather, will you?" said the father, addressing me.

"Godfather? most willingly, my good fellow; I certainly will be godfather."

"And you will name the boy?"

"Noël, why not? We will call him Noël; it is the very name for a Christmas child."

"Noël, that's it; it will go perfectly with my family name, which is Toussaint." *

We arranged matters as fittingly as possible. The doctor officiated, of course; and I took my role of godfather most seriously, assisted by an agreeable godmother, the mother of the sick woman.

I see you smile; well, perhaps, I looked,

---
* All Saints' Day.

In a Snow Storm

rather grotesque in my new character, but if you had been there, you could not have smiled. When the water of regeneration trickled on the forehead of the little being, so frail, so helpless, whose life, by a most wonderful interposition of Providence, we had probably saved, at its very entrance into this world, you could not help turning your thoughts back from this humble home to the sacred stable of Bethlehem. And this impression was so real to me, that it seemed as though I actually heard the voices of the shepherds of old, when our comrade Pierre, who had gone back to the stable to finish his duties, set his foot on the threshold of the door, giving forth, amid the booming of the tempest, the first notes of the old carol: "*Les anges dans nos campagnes—*"

We fell on our knees, and for my part—why should I deny it?—I felt a big tear

Christmas in French Canada

running down my cheek, which I did not even attempt to conceal.

But the ceremony did not end there. Pierre's journey to the stable had not had the interest of his horses for its only end. His Norman sagacity had smelt out the contents of the hamper he had seen us tuck away beneath the seat of the cariole ; and making the judicious reflection that what was good for the *curé* could not be bad for his parishioners, he concluded with sound logic that the midnight watch at the presbytery of St. Tite having been unavoidably missed, it would be absurd not to utilize the good things elsewhere.

Upon this, as his frozen fingers had recovered their normal circulation, he had simply brought the hamper to the house, and when we noticed the fact, the table was already prepared for the feast.

One can imagine the explosion of gayety which followed.

All Pierre's couplets and refrains were gone through, accompanied by the clinking of the glasses, and sustained by the majestic

"*All Pierre's couplets and refrains were gone through*"

Page 40

In a Snow Storm

voice of the storm, roaring and thundering in the distance.

I have enjoyed the Christmas *fête* in France, in England and in this country, at my house and at the houses of others; well, the remembrance of the finest feast I ever sat down to cannot obliterate the memory of that joyful repast, and the merry toast we drank that night to the health of this humble son of peasants, dozing beside his happy mother under the roof of a miserable cottage, isolated in the mountains and shaken in the raging grasp of a northern hurricane.

LITTLE PAULINE

LITTLE PAULINE, little Pauline, why, so young and already an unbeliever!

You do not believe any more in Santa Claus...

Neither in the bogie man, of course—the one being the complement of the other.

Already indifferent to infantine legends! What will it be, when you are twenty, when you begin to discover what amount of deception life keeps in store for the hearts fond of fanciful illusions?

Had she learned the fact through her elder brother, or had the little maid found it out herself at the previous Christmas?

Half awake in her little white couch, had

Little Pauline

she treacherously spied, by the dim reflection of the night lamp, her mamma stealing silently towards the fire-place, where the small shoes awaited the passage of Santa Claus?

At all events, little Pauline had lost her childish faith.

Little Pauline, little Pauline, beware; once on the path of scepticism, where shall you stop?

Farewell to the radiant visions which make you smile in your sleep!

Farewell to the beautiful floating angels who lull you in their arms, and refresh your brow with the fanning of their long silken feathers!

Farewell to the first illusions!

Little Pauline, little Pauline, God spare you the others!

Little Pauline was a charming lass of five years, blonde and pretty, with soft and dreaming eyes, very tall for her age, who could read well enough already, sing a song at the piano, and dance a minuet with exquisite gracefulness.

When she balanced herself, her waist

Christmas in French Canada

elegantly cambered, the point of her foot projected forward, and her skirt open like a fan in the gentle pressure of her delicate fingers, the father had a happy smile, the mother was ravished with admiration, and "Aunt Lucy," crazy with pride, would seize the child like a prey, enveloping her in a jealous and rapturous caress.

Who was Aunt Lucy?

Aunt Lucy, who, by the way, had of an aunt only the name... and tenderness, was the widow of a man whom she adored, and who worshipped her, but had left her childless.

She possessed enough to insure her independence; but, almost without relatives, she had found herself condemned to comparative loneliness, when a young married couple, hearty friends of the departed one, invited her to spend some time in their comfortable and happy home.

When she talked of leaving, they would not let her go.

Little Pauline

Her good nature, her delicate disposition of mind, her advice always dictated by the soundest judgment, together with any amount of petty services of all kind, had made her the benevolent genius of the house.

She had grown indispensable ; she became one of the family.

In the meantime, little Pauline was born.

Useless to tell who was the godmother.

Aunt Lucy eagerly took possession of the baby, which henceforth had two mothers.

The role of the nurse became a sinecure.

The true mother herself had one only privilege, that of offering her breast.

This stranger, who had never known the felicity and ecstasies of maternity began to cherish that child with all the virginal love treasured up in her heart.

Her worship for the husband, all the affection, all the devotion, all the idolatry she would have had for children of her own if God had given her any, all was conveyed upon that sweet little blonde head, who smiled to her old days with an ineffable expression of gratitude.

Christmas in French Canada

For children, as is the case with certain beings deprived of judgment, if they have not the intuition of life to a degree which permits them to reason about their feelings, have at least the instinct of them, and little Pauline, probably without realizing the immensity of such an affection, gave love for love to the old friend who had eyes only for her.

Little Pauline grew up, we may say, in the shadow of Aunt Lucy.

And both, the rosy baby and she who could have been her grandmother, became inseparable.

At night, the two bedsteads, the large and the small one, were side by side.

At table, Aunt Lucy gave the beakfull to little Pauline, who turned around from time to time to caress her old friend's cheek with her small rosy nailed hand, or interrupted her meal to pass her arms around the good lady's shoulder like a graceful necklace.

The child followed Aunt Lucy everywhere, sat by her side to lull the big doll, held her hand while passing from one room to the other, entertained her with inexhaustible

Little Pauline

chattering, or, while the embroidery or the net-work was going on, amused herself by humming fragments of melodies like a nightingale in a bush.

If little Pauline ever perceived she was alone, "Aunt Lucy!" she cried with anxiety.

There is always some one to tease children; if any body ventured to say: "You know, little Pauline, Aunty Lucy is going away!" little Pauline would raise her eyes with alarm, her face would take an expression of supreme distress, and the sweet smile of her dear little lips would contract into a convulsive expression prelusive to a sob.

Pauline.

One had to hasten with: "No, no, darling! no, darling, it's all for fun!" or else the poor little one would burst into tears.

Her brow resumed at once its calmness,

Christmas in French Canada

but her little breast still throbbed a while, like that of a wounded bird.

But Christmas was coming.

Christmas boxes, New Year's gifts, presents of all kinds were freely talked of.

Little Pauline's eyes sparkled, questioning those of Aunt Lucy, whose crow's foot wrinkled in a mysterious and good smile full of alluring promises and joyful forebodings.

"If little Pauline behaves like a good girl," said Aunt Lucy, "if she says her prayers well and retires early, after having hung up her stockings at the foot of her bed, and left her pretty new shoes in the chimney corner, sure enough, Santa Claus, who is the good Jesus' messenger, will come down this night and fill them up with candies, dolls and toys."

"With his long white beard?"

"Yes, love."

"With his big pointed hat?"

"Yes, my beauty."

"And his nice fur mantle?"

"Yes, my treasure."

Little Pauline

"And his large basket?"

"Yes, darling, full of beautiful presents for the good babies who go to bed early and say their prayers well."

"Ah! Ah! Ah!.."

And the pearly laugh of little Pauline burst out fresh and ringing, like a gurgling of a silver stream, while, her forehead surrounded by a wreath of curl-papers, and her feet entangled in the folds of her white-laced night robe, she knelt before Aunt Lucy with a cunning wink full of provoking incredulity.

"And you, Aunty," said she, "are you also going to hang your stockings at the foot of your bed, and put your new boots on the hearth-stone?"

"Nonsense!"

"Why not?"

"My stockings and my boots are too big; Santa Claus will see very well that they are not baby things."

"Put them there anyhow!"

"What for?"

"To please little Pauline."

Christmas in French Canada

Ah! well, since it pleases little Pauline, Aunt Lucy will obey; it is written!

And here are Aunt Lucy's stockings hanging at the bars of her brass bedstead, and her slippers ranged near the andirons, side by side with the new shoes of little Pauline, who hides her blonde head in her pillows, quivering and laughing like a tickled baby, with the same sly and perfidious expression of face.

Little Pauline, little Pauline, you conceal some mischief; what kind of plot are you meditating?

There you are, closing your eyes, and pretending to sleep; what waggish trick are you scheming, little Pauline?

Every evening, after prayer and night toilet, Aunt Lucy used to sit down by the cot, hold little Pauline's hand in her own, and talk the child to sleep by relating to her Cinderella, the Sleeping Beauty, and Aladdin's Lamp, or some other fairy tales which told of beautiful princesses all sparkling with jewels, drawn by quadrigas of gold horned gazelles, in mother-of-pearl carriages

Little Pauline

rolling on wheels glittering with diamonds and rubies.

Some other time she would sing, endeavoring to imitate, as much as possible, the accent of Gascony, the facetious song of Nadaud:

> *Si la Garonne avait voulu,*
> *Lanturlu...*

The little one laughed heartily, and more than once fell asleep murmuring:

> *La Galonne... Lantulu...*

But that evening little Pauline asked for neither the daily fairy tale, nor Nadaud's song.

It appears she had something else in mind.

She was thinking, the little rogue! she was thinking, opening now and then just the corner of an eye, to see if Aunt Lucy was soon, herself, going to sleep.

She was thinking under her curtains, trembling like a poor anxious turtle-dove, eyes and ears on the look-out, watching—the little spy!—a kind of vague rummage

Christmas in French Canada

and smothered noise which came from mamma's bed-room, next to Aunt Lucy's.

At last Aunt Lucy is asleep, as indicates her longer and more accentuated respiration.

Aunt Lucy sleeps; and little Pauline, who is aware of it, outlines a cunning smile, and doubtless to be in a better position to hear and see, and resist at the same time the sleepiness which threatens to take possession of her also, she raises her fair head and gracefully leans it upon her plump little hand, and with her elbow sinking in her pillow, waits in expectancy.

What is she waiting for?

Suddenly some footsteps are heard, or rather guessed; and little Pauline, whose heart beats rapidly, thrusts herself back under her blankets, restless, in the soft and silky feathers, with her eyes well closed up, and her mouth half opened for a smile, just like a child who had been sound asleep for an hour.

Ah! little Pauline, little Pauline, what a hypocrite you are...!

All dressed in white and glad-looking, like

Little Pauline

those charming phantoms who sometimes pass through our youthful dreams, the mother has stealthily entered the room; she throws a long glance to her child, gazes with gratitude at the sweet and kind friend who has made herself the guardian angel of the dear little one, and then wiping a tear of happiness which has glided over her cheek, she stoops one moment before the pretty stockings hanging at the foot of little Pauline's bed.

. . .   . . .

She has left now; gone towards the drawing room where stands the chimney through which Santa Claus is to come; and soon she returns, passing, all white and smiling, in front of the room where little Pauline peeps out, white and smiling also, in the vague and soft glimmer of the night lamp.

And what then?

Ah! little Pauline, you are a terrible rogue; but what a delicious picture you make thus, in that dim light while slipping out of your bed, frightened and shivering, alone with your eyes open in the darkness of this big silent house!

Christmas in French Canada

What is she doing?

No doubt she is going to taste the candies her mamma has dropped into the little stockings. She is too impatient to wait till morning to admire the toys and especially the sparkish doll under which her new shoes must be buried; it is quite natural.

But no, far from it.

She hardly looks at the candies.

They rapidly pass through her hands; to go where?

Not far; right into the stockings of Aunt Lucy, who is sound asleep.

The shares are quickly made. Little Pauline does not take the trouble of counting; and when Aunt Lucy gets up in the morning, she will have no reason to complain of her lot.

But this is not all.

Where are you going now, little Pauline? Are you not afraid of the black dog, crossing that dark and lonely parlor?

Yes, she is; she trembles, trembles, the poor thing; but she walks right through all the same, and then hastens back, after having

Little Pauline

knelt down a moment in front of the big fire-place.

To-morrow, Aunt Lucy, as well as little Pauline, will find lots of nice presents crammed in her boots.

And little Pauline, with gleeful heart, returns quietly, quietly to her bed, and falls asleep with her face turned towards her who will weep to-morrow in discovering the touching fraud, the sacred treachery of the little heroine she loves more than life.

And now, little Pauline, you do not hear the sonorous peals of the church bells chiming in the night.

You do not hear the sacred hymns floating in the illuminated sanctuaries, nor the harmonies of the great organs roaring and thundering under the arches of the lofty vaults.

You do not see, from your downy little bed, the pious crowd kneeling around the manger in which the Infant-Jesus outstretches his little arms towards the pious and kneeling crowd.

No, but surely the good angels who

Christmas in French Canada

looked at you this evening from the altitudes where they sang: "Glory to God in Heaven, and peace on Earth to men of good-will," have descended towards you, my little Pauline, and now bend their heads over the white couch where you sleep, to kiss your brow, and bless your little great heart.

"To kiss your brow and bless your little great heart"

Page 112

To kiss your brow and bless your little great heart

THE CHRISTMAS LOG

"GRANDMAMMA, tell us a story, please."

"A story, a story, grandmamma!"

"A Christmas story."

"The story of the Man in the Moon. You promised to tell it."

And the pretty heads, fair and dark, with opened mouths and sparkling eyes, gathered around the rocking-

Christmas in French Canada

chair of grandmamma, who, her spectacles on her nose, after treating herself to a pinch of Spanish snuff, took her net-work, threw a glance around, which brought a smile on her wrinkled lips, dropped her woollen ball into the apron of the youngest, began to move her knitting-needles rapidly with her long and slender fingers, and then commenced in a slightly quivering voice:

"Once upon a time, my children. . ."

At this moment, there was a stir amongst the listeners. Everyone moved in his place; the tallest gave a little cough; the most attentive leaned forward with elbows on knees and chin in hands; then there was a hush, and everyone began to listen with mouth, eyes and ears.

"Once upon a time, my children," repeated the old lady as she went on with her knitting, "there was an old château, very old indeed, very gloomy and solitary, standing on the rocky flank of a hill crowned by a forest of large oaks, and named the castle of Kerfoël.

"I mean that this was its real name, for it was better known in the country as the Devil's Tower.

The Christmas Log

"In fact it was said that, in old days, the Devil had built a forge and furnace in one of the highest rooms of the turret, where he made gold for the owners of the domain, who, for his services, belonged to him from generation to generation.

"There must have been some evil source for the wealth of these wretched miscreants, for, from the top of their towers, one could make out nothing but barren and dry moors planted here and there with big fairy-stones, standing up like men, which are called in Brittany menhirs or Satan's distaffs.

"For I must tell you, my children, that the story I am about to tell took place in France, in the old province called Brittany, where the grandmother of my own grandmother came from, when our people settled in this land of America.

"Well, in the days I am speaking of, the lord of Kerfoël, the owner of the Devil's Tower, was named Robert. He was crippled from birth—bandy-legged and club-footed, and this deformity, which did not prevent his being as strong as a giant, had not lightly con-

Christmas in French Canada

tributed to the diabolical reputation he had gained by his ill-tempered, ungoverned and thoroughly bad character.

"Brought up like a heathen, he had passed his youth hunting wild boars in the woods—even on Sundays and other holy days—harrying the poor peasants, blaspheming the name of God, and indulging in all sorts of wickedness. He was never seen in church; he never uncovered his head before the Calvaries he passed on his way; he shamelessly ate meat on Fridays, and laughed with impudence at funerals.

"People pretended they had seen him at night, limping on his twisted leg far away on the moor, in company with the great big stones I told you of, which followed him like dogs in the moonlight, without anybody being able to tell where he was going. In short, the Count Robert de Kerfoël was a wretched sinner, fearing neither God nor Satan, sneering at holy things, and although quite young yet, had by this impious and sacrilegious conduct caused his mother's death from a broken heart. As to his father, whose

The Christmas Log

life had hardly been better than his son's, he had died—without confession—in a corner of the forest, where his body had been found half-devoured by wolves.

"It was a sad end, indeed, but the son was to finish still more miserably, as you shall see."

No interruption was to be heard in the little group; on the contrary not even a finger moved; every word, every syllable was snapped up, and the attention of the small audience increased as the good old lady went on with her narrative:

"You have seen the man in the moon, have you not, my children?"

"Yes, grandmamma."

"A lame man."

"Who is going down hill."

"With a bundle of straw on his shoulders."

"No, a faggot."

"A log, children, a burning log. One can see him clearly at night, when the stars glitter in the sky and when the full moon rolls her silvery disk between us and the blue depths of the firmament; especially on the holy

Christmas in French Canada

Christmas night, when Santa Claus goes from house to house with his presents for the good little children; when the church windows mingle their rosy glare with the pale lights which fall from Heaven on the snow-covered hills; you have seen him, have you not?"

"Yes, yes, grandmamma."

"With the log on his shoulder."

"Yes, and with his crooked leg."

"Well, listen, now."

And the little circle pressed once more around the rocking chair, while grandmamma continued:

"In Brittany—the valiant land of Brittany—in that good old fatherland of our forefathers, Christmas was not celebrated as it is here, where we simply attend midnight mass, and drink a glass of liquor, nibbling a branch of *croquignole* sprinkled with powdered sugar. There, it was the peasants' day, the feast of the poor, and the country festival above all others.

"The folk gathered in the châteaux and large farm houses; and there young and old

The Christmas Log

waited for midnight mass with all manner of rejoicing.

"First, they had what was called the 'Christmas log,' a huge fragment cut from the trunk of a tree, prepared and well dried beforehand, which was burnt in the great chimney place, after having been baptized by dropping over it a brimmer of wine from the last vintage; after which they sang the old carols, and feasted with cider and *nieulles*.

"Nieulles, you know, were crusty little cakes baked for Christmas only. No Christmas was complete without them.

"So they used to crunch nieulles; *crunch nieulles*, you understand. Evidently the origin of our *croquignoles*.

"And they danced. Ah! well, our forefathers had not fine pianos as we have to-day. The violin itself was still unknown in the villages of Brittany. No waltzes, nor quadrilles, nor even cotillions. Boys and girls danced the *bourrée* and the *carole* to the sound of the *biniou*, an instrument something like the bagpipes you have seen with the Scotch regiments.

Christmas in French Canada

"No floors brilliantly waxed, either, my children; nor Oriental carpets, nor elegant shining pumps. But people did not enjoy it the less for that, I fancy; at all events, it was not the harmonious *clic-clac* of the beech-tree shoes on the resounding flagstones that could spoil the music.

"As you can easily imagine, my pets, the Holy Christmas was not celebrated in this fashion at the Devil's tower.

"The people at the château on that night did but as we do here; they simply went to church to adore the divine Infant in his manger, and returned silently to gather around the hearth, where the old gamekeeper Le Goffic, like your grandmammas to-day, used to relate some old story, or sing some old carol, but in a very low voice, of course, for fear of being overheard by the master.

"And it was thus, over and over from one season to another, the years following in sadness and fear, without a moment of gayety, without a glimmer of joyousness.

"One morning it happened that Count

The Christmas Log

Robert sent for his steward, Yvon Kerouak, and had a long talk with him. Then he ordered his best steed to be saddled, and with a heavy travelling bag well buckled on the croup, he started away without saying a word to a living soul.

"Where did he go? Nobody ever knew.

" Months followed weeks, and years months, without bringing the slightest news of him. After a long while he was supposed to be dead, and everyone made the sign of the cross on his breast with his thumb on hearing the name of the Count de Kerfoël, who must have been the victim of some dreadful punishment, and who surely would never be seen again in this life, and, if it pleased God, in the other either.

"Twenty years had gone by. The steward, the housekeeper, and other servants had grown grey; the old watchman Le Goffic counted over eighty years; and everyone having become convinced that the absentee would never return, a more peaceful life had introduced itself by degrees, if not under the lofty ceilings of the state rooms, at least under

Christmas in French Canada

the smoked rafters of the common hall, where the peasants and shepherds of the neighborhood occasionally gathered on public festivals or days of rest, to enjoy themselves.

"In short, thanks to the disappearance of Count Robert, the inhabitants of the old château had begun to lead a more quiet and happy life; and merry times became as frequent at the Devil's Tower as anywhere else.

"Especially on Christmas Eve was there joyful merry making and abundant feasting under the battlements of the old Tower, which might not have failed, in time, to acquire a Christian reputation, if the tragical event I am going to relate had not added its fantastic page to the old legend.

"One year the inhabitants of the château had made up their minds to celebrate Christmas Eve with exceptional splendor. A huge billet cut out of one of the giant oaks of the park had been prepared for the ceremony; and, as early as eight o'clock in the evening, all the neighbors, the biniou-player heading, crowded into the large hall of the château,

The Christmas Log

illuminated by rosin torches and the lively blaze which already caressed the Christmas log proudly installed right in the centre of the hearth.

"The foaming cider was passed around, stimulating joyous repartees and provoking explosions of laughter among the feasters; and each one swallowed his bumper to the ringing of the rustic goblets, while, and through all, droned the long and snuffling notes of the biniou.

"Suddenly:

"'Noël! Noël!..' cried all the voices in one enthusiastic acclamation which made the old Gothic windows with their colored and leaded panes tinkle. The Christmas log had just taken fire, crackling and spreading all about showers of brilliant sparks.

"'The baptism! the baptism!' cried everyone.

"'Uncle Le Goffic! to you the honors of the ceremony!'

"'Come, baptize the Christmas log, uncle Le Goffic!'

"'Uncle Le Goffic! uncle Le Goffic!'

Christmas in French Canada

"And all fell on their knees, while the old game-keeper, with bare head, advanced towards the large fire-place, whose light shone like a glory around his long white hair, outlining as on a golden background, the majestic and imposing figure of the old man.

"'*In the name of the Father, and of the Son, and of the Holy Ghost!*' said he in a low and solemn tone, while his knotty and trembling hand dropped a ruby-like string of wine on the heavy fragment of oak bitten by the winding blaze.

"The bystanders had not time to answer *amen*, before a wild gust of wind swept aside the flames of the hearth, and in the opened door stood the evil and deformed figure of Count Robert de Kerfoël.

"Everyone stood up, dumb and horrified. After a moment of deadly silence, the new-comer threw a ferocious glance about, and with a drawn sword, advanced through the terrified peasants towards the chimney.

"'*Par la mort Dieu!*' cried he with a haughty and thundering voice, 'since when has my dwelling become the scene of such

Christening the Christmas Log

Page 124

The Christmas Log

ridiculous mummeries? . . Joël,' added he, as he turned towards his old groom and pointed to the blazing fire, 'throw away this emblem of a cursed superstition!'

"An exclamation of terror followed:

"'The Christmas log?'

"'Yes, the Christmas log, out of this with it! Do you hear me, Joël?

"'My Lord Count,' replied Joël, kneeling down in fear, 'the Christmas log is sacred: I'd rather die than touch it.'

"The count Robert was crazy with rage.

"'By all the devils!' yelled he, addressing the steward, whom he had just detected in the crowd, 'who commands here, Yvon Kerouak?'

"'My Lord Count,' replied the steward, 'the Christmas log is hallowed; to touch it would be a crime!'

"'It would be a crime!' repeated all like an echo.

"At this the exasperation of the miscreant knew no bounds.

"'Stupid idiots!' cried he.

"And then, laying hold of two jugs of

Christmas in French Canada

cider, he emptied them over the burning log, and pulled the same with his own hands out of the fire-place, and lifted it to his shoulder without regard to the firebrands which singed his hair and shrivelled his skin.

"'My Lord Count,' besought the old game-keeper, shivering from head to foot, 'the Christmas log has been baptized, beware of God's hand, my Lord Count!'

"'Sacrilege!' exclaimed several voices, as limping in a dreadful fashion, his back bent under the weight of the smoking billet, the Cóunt stepped across the threshold, and, with horrible blasphemies, disappeared in the outside darkness.

"'Let us kneel down!' cried old Le Goffic.

"But it was too late; a terrible cry of distress, which had in it nothing human, sounded in the night, raising up the hair of all the witnesses of the terrible scene.

"And never again was the Count Robert de Kerfoël, the last Lord of the Devil's Tower, seen amongst the living.

"Ever since that night, my children, one

The Christmas Log

can see on the shining disk of the moon, in clear weather, a man with a twisted knee, stooping under a strange burden in which those who see clearly enough can make out a half-burnt log still flaming here and there.

"The unfortunate Count Robert is condemned to carry the burden on his shoulder until the day of the last judgment."

"And it is he we see in the moon, grand-mamma?"

"They say so, my children."

"With the Christmas log?"

"Yes, my children."

"With his crooked leg?"

"And his club-foot?"

"Yes."

"Is that story true?" asked one of the urchins, who had listened most attentively and with the most widely opened eyes.

"Pshaw!" said the tallest of the girls; "a fairy tale."

"Well, of course, my children," said the grandmother, smilingly, "you asked me for a Christmas story. I have related you what was related to me when I was a child; you

Christmas in French Canada

may do the same in your turn when you are old; let your listeners believe if they wish."

Jeannette.

JEANNETTE, a chubby little maid, roly-poly and plump, with inviting dimples and wary black eyes, had, at first—oh! immediately! almost from birth—shown an instinctive antipathy for her father.

When he leaned over her cradle with a kiss on his lips, she would outline a grimace of dislike at him, and if he opened his arms

Christmas in French Canada

for an embrace, she would turn to her mother with outstretched hands, as if to implore help.

A painful circumstance, which changed the face of things, came to console him.

Jeannette fell ill.

During several days, a devouring fever hollowed her cheeks, dulled her eyes, and, so to speak, gnawed her thin and shivering little limbs.

The father did his best to encourage his wife in despair. When the poor mother took a little rest, he in his turn sat at the bed-side of the little one, and bending over her with tear-dimmed eyes, heavy-hearted and dejected, he almost imprecated his powerlessness to relieve the dear child for whose health he would so willingly have given his own, a thousand times.

One morning Jeannette opened her eyes at the very moment when a heavy tear splashed on her poor, pale, helpless little hand.

She had the strength to turn her head toward her father; and then, these two beings so different in age and in nature, exchanged one of those looks that are never forgotten,

Jeannette

and by which is sometimes effected that transfusion of souls, that only those who are made to love passionately can understand.

The father had conquered the heart of his child; the child had guessed and sounded that of her father.

Convalescence is rapid with the little ones. The dear invalid took a new lease on life; her cheeks bloomed anew, her large, velvety eyes recovered their pristine brightness, her pretty dimples appeared once more as the lurking-place of sweet kisses, her lips, long mute and livid, found again their smile, their color and their silvery notes.

The house became once more as ringing as a spring day, and as cheerful as a sunbeam.

A revolution had taken place in Jeannette's character; she adored her father.

She was never happier than, when sitting on his knees, she pulled his beard, tickled his neck, or teased him with a thousand coaxing caresses, while she prattled as uninterruptedly as a finch on a marauding expedition.

On his side, never was the father more beaming with joy than when he rocked the

Christmas in French Canada

arch little lass in his arms, relating to her the adventures of Hop-o'-my-Thumb, or singing to her some ballad of the times of yore.

Do not ask me if they were happy.

But all this is digression.

Jeannette had grown; she was now turned four years, and the affection she had vowed to her father had not diminished.

On the contrary, the little one had become his inseparable companion; and, as long as he was at home, she deafened, or rather charmed him by her chatter, told him a myriad adorable nothings, and asked him a thousand questions which the good papa answered with imperturbable complacency.

At the coming of Christmas, a holiday so impatiently awaited by the little folks, the conversation between the parents and babies runs, naturally enough, on the presents to which this time of the year almost always gives rise in well-to-do families.

This was Jeannette's great preoccupation. The day before Christmas Eve, as the family dinner was drawing to a close, all at once she became pensive, and after a moment's

Jeannette

reflection, during which the graceful curve of her eye-brows had become somewhat marred in the struggle of a confused thought, she said brusquely:

"Tell me, papa, is it the Infant-Jesus or Santa Claus who comes down in the chimney to put presents in the shoes of the little children who have been good?"

"Why do you ask me that?"

"Well, there are some people who say that it is Santa Claus, and others who say it is the Infant-Jesus."

"They both come, my love; each one in turn, each one his year."

"And this year it is the turn of...?"

"Of the Infant-Jesus."

And as the child clapped her hands with a joyous exclamation, the father added:

"You are glad?"

"Oh! yes."

"You love the Infant-Jesus better than Santa Claus?"

"Yes, indeed."

"But why?"

"Because....!"

Christmas in French Canada

And Jeannette put her finger in her mouth with a deliciously provoking expression of face.

"Tell me why," insisted the father; "Santa Claus brought you handsome toys last year."

"Yes."

"With a beautiful big doll."

"Yes."

"Then why don't you love him?"

"Because... he is not good to everybody."

"He is not good to everybody?"

"No; he does not love the little children who are poor; he does not give them anything."

"Are you sure that Santa Claus gives nothing to the poor children?"

"I am; Rosina told me so."

"Who is Rosina?"

"The washerwoman's little girl. I asked her if she was going to put her shoes in the chimney to-morrow night. She said she had put them last year, but that she had found nothing in them, although she had been ever so good. Her mother says that Santa Claus only goes to rich people. But since it is the Infant-Jesus who comes this year, I

Jeannette

will tell Rosina to try again. Little Jesus must love poor people as much as the others, since he was poor himself."

"But are you sure that he will go?"

Jeannette remained a few moments nonplussed; but after a moment's reflection:

"Yes," she said. "He will go. I shall pray him hard, hard, and surely he won't refuse me."

An hour after; softly enveloped in her fresh white night dress, her chin propped upon her primly folded hands, and her knees sunk in the long silky hairs of a llama skin rug, Jeannette prayed like a little angel that she was; then while the mother gave her the good night kiss, and tucked in warmly the covering of the little bed, the name of Rosina passed like a sigh on the lips of the sleeping child.

When the morning sun stained with pink the window of the room where she slept, Jeannette rose absorbed in thought. Her father's last words "Are you sure that he will go?" returned to her memory, and the child began not to be so sure of the efficacy of her prayer.

Christmas in French Canada

"After all, perhaps he will not go," she said to herself. And this supposition saddened her almost to tears.

"What is the matter with you this morning, my Jeannette," said the father; "you are not so gay as usual. Don't you know that to-night is Christmas Eve, and that, since you have been very good, to-morrow morning your little shoes, and even your little stockings perhaps, will be crammed with pretty things?"

Jeannette smiled, but remained pensive.

"Papa," she said as though she had suddenly come to a decision, "if I knew how to write .... but I can only sign my name."

"What would you do if you could write?"

"I would write a letter."

"To whom?"

"To little Jesus."

"Well, my love, tell me what you want to tell the Infant-Jesus; I will write to him, and you will sign."

"Truly?"

"At once, if you want."

"And it will be the same thing?"

"Exactly the same."

"Dictated word for word by his spoilt pet"
Page 136

Jeannette

"Oh! dear good papa!"

And the little one threw herself into the arms of the "dear good papa," who, a few minutes after, was sitting at his desk writing the following letter dictated word for word by his spoilt pet:

DEAR LITTLE JESUS,

"To-morrow is your feast of Christmas, and as I have been very good, I put my shoes on the hearthstone, just like the other children. But give me only your picture, and take the presents to Rosina who is very good also, but whose mother is a poor widow. You know her house, don't you? It's on Sanguinet street. There is a big tree right in front—"

Here Jeannette jumped.

A big tear, similar to the one that had wakened her one day by falling on her sick little hand, had just wet the paper, where the father's nervous fingers had some difficulty in following the lines.

"Why do you cry?" she asked, passing a pudgy little arm around his neck and looking tenderly into his eyes.

Too much moved to answer, the good father took his child in his arms, pressed her

Christmas in French Canada

closely to his heart, enveloping her in a lasting passionate embrace; and for a long, long time, he jealously contemplated his treasure through the tears of happiness and love that filled his eyes.

When the little one had scribbled her name at the foot of her touching letter to the Infant-Jesus, her father stood up and walked up and down for a few minutes to recover himself. Then, with his back turned, he stood for some time before the window of his study, his gaze lost in the brilliant azure of the December sky; and when entering the room, the mother —tenderly loved also—heard him murmur in a half-sob:

"Provided God does not take her away from us...."

At night the naive missive, carefully directed, lay in the little shoe slid behind the fire dogs; and, after having said her prayers as the night before, Jeannette softly fell asleep amid her white laces, to dream of Child Jesus, of the good Angels and of Paradise.

Not far from there, in a humble and lowly

Jeannette

home, at the first glimmer of dawn, a poor little girl—who sometimes accompanied her mother when the latter brought newly-washed clothes to the house of Jeannette's parents—the little Rosina so warmly recommended in the letter to the Infant-Jesus, had a great surprise and a great joy.

Beaming with happiness, she carried to her mother's bedside a pink-cheeked, yellow-haired doll in elaborate costume.

Her old shoes had disappeared, yielding the place in the corner of the chimney to warm and elegant boots in both of which shone a gold coin.

Of course it is unnecessary to add that on the special recommendation of her mother, the child's first visit was to Jeannette.

"Me," said the latter, "I have not a doll, nor new shoes, nor gold pieces, but I have more than all that. The little Jesus gave me his picture. Here it is."

And she ran to get a pretty chromo-lithograph, very brilliantly festooned with gold arabesques, showing the divine Infant in his

Christmas in French Canada

manger. On the back of the picture was inscribed in a superb round hand:

To Jeannette, from the Little Jesus.

"It comes from Him?"

"Yes, I found it in my shoe."

"Oh! how beautiful He is!" cried Rosina enthusiastically.

"Is He not charming?" approved Jeannette.

"And how well He writes!"

"Yes, He writes just like Marius."

By the way, Marius was a valet, whose graphical talent was generally put into requisition when there was some careful writing to be done.

No, Jeannette had no other presents for Christmas that year, but she lost no time by waiting, for papa and mamma took their revenge royally on the New Year.

Jeannette is now nineteen.

She is a tall, handsome brunette, who has made her début at the last St. Catherine ball, and who cherishes her father as much as ever.

Jeannette

Recently she happened to unlock an elegant casket in the presence of one of her friends.

"Here," she said, "this is a picture I have kept since I was a four years old little bit of a thing."

"Really? Oh! the pretty Christ Child."

"Is it not nice?"

"Why don't you put this little jewel among your other knick-knacks?"

"Ah! well, do you see," answered the young girl hesitatingly, "I don't know why, but every time that papa looks at it, it never fails to bring a tear to his eyes."

The Phantom Head

THE traveller of to-day who crosses the St. Lawrence between Quebec and Levis, during the winter season, comfortably seated between decks in the powerful screw steamers which occupy only a few minutes in passing from shore to shore, forcing their way through the drifting floes, untroubled by mist or wind driven snow, can have but a

The Phantom Head

faint idea of what this crossing, in old days, really meant.

The trip was made in heavy canoes, or dug-outs, formed of two large trunks solidly joined by a wide and flat keel of polished oak, turned up at both ends, so that the craft could be used as a sledge when needed.

The captain sat astern, on a small platform where he commanded the manoeuvring, steering with a special paddle; while, at the bow, sometimes standing right on the *pince*—the slender projection of the prow—another fearless fellow explored the passes and watched the false openings.

In the front of the pilot, a certain space was reserved for the passengers lying on the flat bottom, wrapped up and covered with buffalo robes, perfectly protected from the cold, but with hardly the power of moving.

The rest of the canoe was crossed with thin planks, equally spaced, which not only strengthened the craft, but also served as seats for the men, who paddled in time, encouraging themselves with voice and gesture.

Christmas in French Canada

It was a hard calling; and, as the Canadian winters of those times were much more severe than those of ours, it was sometimes a dangerous one.

Every launching of the canoe—that is, every start from the shore—gave a thrill to the sturdiest. Down from the top of the *batture*—(the icy rampart built along the beach by the rising and falling of the tide, and the constant grinding and breaking of the drifting floes)—down from the top of the batture into the dark and swirling waters, the crew hurriedly jumping on board in a desperate entanglement of hands, legs and arms, it was a matter of a few seconds only, but every heart stood still until the flying start was accomplished.

And, *Nage, camarades!* .... *Haut les coeurs!* .... *Les bons petits coeurs!*

Enormous lumps of greenish ice block the way: quick! go for them! There we are! Down with the paddle, shoulder the rope, and, forward again on the frozen surface of the river!

Further on, great masses are crammed and

"It was a hard calling"

Page 144

The Phantom Head

heaped up one upon the other. The passage seems impracticable.... No matter, hoist up the canoe, and forward once more over the obstacle!

A crevice opens before us; it is an abyss perhaps.... Never mind, drive on at all hazards! Wet snow freezes and sticks to the sides of the canoe, impeding our advance: not a moment to lose: roll in! roll in, boys!... And off we are again!

Now it is different; everything gives way all around. It is no longer water; it is no longer ice. Paddling is impossible; no point of support to heave upon; prisoners in the melting snow and the dissolving ice!.... Courage, boys!.... Away, away, altogether! forward, anyhow!....

And the struggle might go on for hours, sometimes even for the whole day.

Oh! yes, it was a hard calling indeed. Victor Hugo has depicted the "Toilers of the Sea." He should have seen the canoe-men of Levis at work!

Christmas in French Canada

II

Some thirty years ago, I happened to be in company with a newly-married couple from Florida, who had been original enough to undertake a wedding journey through Lower Canada in mid-winter.

These travellers, from a country fragrant with magnolia blossom, and oranges ripening in January, found a deep interest in the peculiarities of our winter weather; and as a proof that their wanderings had been planned with the intelligence and sagacity of two lovers in search of the picturesque, it will be sufficient to say that their itinerary included a visit to Quebec and its vicinity, the midnight mass in the old historic cathedral, a slide on the frozen cone of Montmorency, and a moonlight crossing of the St. Lawrence amid the floating ice.

They had reached Levis in the morning of the day before Christmas, and to insure the moonlight crossing, had spent the day at the Victoria Hotel, where, as an old acquaintance of the husband, I had hastened to join them.

The Phantom Head

In the evening, we made ourselves ready, and started for the quarters where the canoemen generally stood waiting for passengers.

"It is fine moonlight, that's true," said one of them, a fellow by the name of Nazaire Jodoin, "but the cold is bitter and the floes run fast, I tell you! If you don't wish to risk a night on the banks of Beaumont, I would advise you not to face the ice before a couple of hours. No canoe will make Pointe-à-Puyseaux with such a current. Old Baron himself would not dare to try it."

"Where is old Baron?"

"At Uncle Vien's, smoking his pipe. But he won't take you across before eleven or half past, take my word for it! You can walk in and warm yourselves until the ebb is over, and by low tide, I'll land you safe and sound in the Cul-de-sac, just as quick as you can desire."

"Well, then," said I to my friends, "wait for me, I will consult with old Baron; he is the oracle in such matters."

"We will go with you," said the young lady.

Christmas in French Canada

"But, madam, remember I am not going into a drawing-room."

"What do I care? We are not looking for luxuries in our crossing of the St. Lawrence this freezing night."

"But those people smoke like volcanoes; you will be suffocated."

"It cannot be worse than our negroes' cabins, I presume."

"Oh! certainly not."

"I am used to that, let us go! I travel not only to see the country, but also its inhabitants."

"All right, then; the fact is, you will see only honest people, somewhat rustic in their manner, but all kind, good-hearted fellows."

I knew the house of old Vien; we entered without knocking, to find ourselves in a large hall surrounded by wooden benches running close to the walls. On these benches, with crossed legs, or elbows on their knees, a score of canoe-men smoked their brown pipes, exchanging from time to time a few words with indifference or good-natured interest.

The Phantom Head

Others, more recently arrived from outside, with frozen boots and soaking beards, dried their leather mittens, striking the floor with their feet, around the huge cast-iron stove which roared away in the centre of the room.

These men, in more or less shabby attire, wore, for the most part, a grey or red flannel shirt under a round jacket made of baracan, corduroy or *étoffe du pays* tightly fastened around the waist by a belt of gaudy colored wool. A fur cap pulled down to their eyes; their trousers half buried in long-legged moccasins were held up on the hip by a well-buckled strap,—suspenders being inconvenient for the handling of the paddle.

There they were, young and old, black-bearded or grey-haired, hardly distinct in the confused lights falling from the tallow candles held on the wall by tin brackets, and which were themselves hardly distinguishable through the smoke of the pipes and the vapor produced by drying clothes.

Two passengers, seated in a corner, awaited, like ourselves, the favorable moment to start.

Christmas in French Canada

III

On our entrance all conversation ceased, and each one uncovered himself, for politeness is traditional with the French Canadian, humble as may be his position in life.

"*Entrez, mam'zelle! entrez, ces messieurs!*" said the master of the house, advancing; "come and seat yourselves. You wish to cross, no doubt?"

"Yes, M. Vien," said I, "and at once if possible. What do you think of it, M. Baron?"

"It is always possible to tempt Providence," sententiously answered a tall old man, white-headed and honest-looking, who

Old Baron

was smoking his short pipe apart from the others, seated on the only chair there was in the room, "it is always possible to tempt Providence, but it does not bring good luck."

"You believe there is a risk?"

The Phantom Head

"There is at least the risk of passing the night on the ice; and with a *créature* (lady), it is not a pleasant thing."

"You can depend on old Baron," intervened our host, "he seldom gives bad advice."

"That's true," said one of the smoking crowd; "if poor Sanschagrin had listened to him, last year, he would probably be still in the world."

"Well," said one of the canoe men who had not spoken yet—a man with a gloomy air and a long black beard—"he had seen Peter's head, you understand; and when a fellow has seen Peter's head . . . ."

"He is bound to perish within a year," added one of his comrades.

"Gracious me! if I had the misfortune to see such a thing," said another voice, "I wouldn't board a canoe for a thousand!"

"I wouldn't touch a paddle for a fortune!" added another fellow.

"Nor I, surely!" exclaimed several listeners.

"A legend?" whispered my friend's wife, to whom the good old man had courteously

Christmas in French Canada

offered the only chair in the hall, "a legend? It is a godsend; pray, have them tell us the story."

"What do you mean by Peter's head?" said I to the man who had first alluded to the matter.

"Friend Baron can tell you about that better than I," said the man of gloomy appearance, "the thing happened in his days."

"Sure enough!" said old Vien; "Baron knew Peter Soulard well, and so did I. A young man of good character, but not lucky.

"If he was not lucky," said old Baron, "he was not very prudent either, the poor devil! Take my word, *mes gars*, it is very well to be brave and valiant, but one must not tempt Providence. One never repents of having been too cautious, while he often regrets not having been cautious enough. I don't like to boast, but I have paddled across the St. Lawrence in winter, spring, and autumn, in all kinds of weather, almost every day of my life, and I never met with the slightest accident. Why? Because I never played the braggart, and always hated

"At Uncle Vien's"

The Phantom Head

bravado. I was not scared by trifles, certainly not; but I was never ashamed to withdraw before a real danger. One can risk his own life if he wishes, when not stopped by the fear of God, but the lives of others are not to be played with. Unfortunately poor Peter Soulard was more courageous than prudent. He preferred facing any danger than to be suspected of cowardice."

And old Baron, yielding to enthusiastic recollections, told us the story of Peter Soulard.

IV

The story takes us back to January, 1844.

The winter was exceptionally severe. Almost uninterrupted easterly winds had blown over the region of Quebec, blizzard upon blizzard, in rolling avalanches of hail and blinding snow, which made the crossing of the river most difficult and sometimes impossible.

The tide drifted, from morning till night, and from night till morning, mountains of ice which broke furiously on the angles of

Christmas in French Canada

the wharves with tremendous crash. It was only at intervals that the eye could reach from one shore to the other, through the heavy fogs tormented by the squalls.

The life was hard for the poor canoe-men. When they left their homes in the morning, they were not always sure to be back at night.

One day, however, the sun had risen on a clear and calm atmosphere. The cold was sharp, but dry. One could hear the ice-floes creaking in the distance, and the snow, hardened by the frost, cracked under the feet; but the sky shone, limpid and transparent like blue rock crystal.

The flocs had gathered so abundantly during the night, that they had frozen into a solid mass, closing the outlet of the Quebec basin at the place where the river suddenly narrows, between Point Levis and the southwest end of the Island of Orleans. To use the technical expression: "the ice bridge was frozen at the key."

Now, when the ice bridge freezes at the key, the rest of the floes which come from

The Phantom Head

above are still driven up and down by the current, so that the rising tide thrusts them several miles backwards, until the ebb drives them down against the formidable barrier. This is called the "Chariot."

When the chariot is up above, the river between Quebec and Levis is clear, and the crossing is just as free as in summer time; but beware when the gigantic mass, filling the space from shore to shore, runs down to hurl itself against the rampart that bars its way to the Gulf! The impact is terrible. Woe to those who are caught in the jaws of the blind monster!

As already stated, the weather was exceptionally fine, but the river was no less threatening. Peter Soulard, who commanded a canoe of his own, had crossed from Levis to Quebec early in the morning; and after having loaded his homeward cargo, was preparing for his return to the south shore.

Unfortunately, one of his passengers had caused him to lose much precious time, and the chariot, driven down by the ebbing tide,

Christmas in French Canada

was already doubling the Foulon's wharves, when Peter Soulard, his paddle in his hand, cried out with all the might of his lungs:

"All aboard! all aboard! *Embarque! embarque!*"

"It is late, Peter!" remarked some one.

"Don't bother me, please; I know what I am about."

"Your canoe is too heavily loaded," observed another; "you will have the chariot on you before you can reach Point Levis."

"Mind your own business!" was the only reply. "Do you take me for a greenhorn?"

"Peter," called old Baron himself, who happened to be near by, "no tom-foolery my friend; there is nothing to be gained by tempting Providence."

"You are a set of old women," cried out Peter Soulard, launching his canoe from the top of the batture of the Champlain Market.

It was a heavy plunge in a resounding gush of foam; the paddles strenuously dipped into the waves; and the canoe, manned by

The Phantom Head

sixteen passengers and crew, shot away, under the blue sky, leaving a long silvery track in the dark waters behind, while the cheery shout of Peter Soulard rang out bravely:

"Paddle on, my hearties! *Nageons, nos gens!*"

The tide ran with extreme violence; in a few moments, they were out of sight in the direction of the West India pier.

Twenty minutes later, the roaring chariot was opposite Quebec, and the idlers, who watched the torrent dashing along, saw old Baron stealthily crossing himself, with his eyes turned offward.

That evening, when the early night of January spread its darkness over the hills of Levis, two men were seen walking along the ice-covered beach, sobbing and shaken by convulsive shiverings. It was Peter Soulard, who had escaped from death as by a miracle, with one of his comrades. The other fourteen had perished—drowned in the tumultuous waters, or ruthlessly crushed beneath the onward rush of the savage mass.

Christmas in French Canada

Strange to say, the terrible lesson, frightful as it was, was of no avail to the reckless man. Two years later, his habitual imprudence brought to a fatal end two more unfortunates who ventured to embark with him, in spite of the reputation of fatalism naturally attached to his person.

But this time it was the end of him also, and a most tragical one, too.

While clinging to the flank of his canoe, which had capsized in mid-stream, a rapidly running floe of ice, thin and sharp as a steel blade, struck him a fair blow in the neck, and cut his head clear from his shoulders, in full sight of his horrified companions, as swiftly as would have done the fatal knife of the guillotine itself.

The head of the unfortunate man bounded offward, and slid by starts, leaving behind a dreadful trace of blood upon the ice.

In that dangerous part of the Quebec basin, known as "*entre les deux églises*," between the two churches of St. Joseph and Beauport, especially in foggy or snow-drifting weather, the horrible head sometimes

The Phantom Head

appears to the terrified crew led astray in those perilous waters.

Suddenly, they see, emerging from the milky darkness, a huge slab of floating ice on which rolls and bounds a black and shapeless object hardly distinguishable in the shifting light.

It is Peter Soulard's head.

Then, about! about! without losing a second! Woe to those who have seen the spectre: they must die within the year, and generally by a sudden and tragical death.

It was said poor Octave Sanschagrin had once been in such a crew.

V

Old Baron was at this point in his story, when a loud voice resounded outside:

"All aboard! all aboard!"

Instantly all the canoe-men were on their feet.

"It's low tide; water still; come on!"

"How many passengers?"

"Five."

Christmas in French Canada

"One canoe and eight good paddlers will be enough."

"Hurry up, it's your turn, Nazaire."

"And it's lucky for you," said I, "for you are going to take across a newly married couple."

"You don't say!"

"Yes, and who see the St. Lawrence for the first time."

"Is that so?"

"Yes, it will bring you luck."

"Ah! well, then, if such be the case, listen to me: I have a brand new craft which I intended to hansel on New Year's day; why not hansel her to-night?"

"That's an idea!" said old Baron; "is she ready?"

"She has only to be taken out of the shed and launched."

"Get her out, then."

"You order so?"

"Of course! We shall christen her like a three-master."

"Will the little lady consent to be god-mother?"

The Phantom Head

"I should think so!" I exclaimed, "and her husband will be godfather. As to me, if you will allow, I shall furnish the liquid. Is that right?"

"That's right!"

"Hurrah!"

"Well then, forward, hearties! .... Ho! ...."

We started, and soon the elegant new craft, dressed up with flags, and with a joyous crew—some at the rope and others at the gunwale—slid along the sloping path which led to the river. A few moments were sufficient to reach the beach.

Old Baron accompanied us.

"Uncle Edouard," said Nazaire Jodoin, addressing him; "you shall come with us, won't you? You shall command; it will be another good omen for my canoe."

Old Baron never hesitated when called upon to perform a task of any kind.

"As you wish, boys!" said he, "but since we are going to baptize a new Christian, have you thought of choosing a name for her?"

"In fact, we must choose a name."

Christmas in French Canada

"Well," said somebody, "it is Christmas Eve—*Noël* in French—why shouldn't we call her *Noël?*"

"No, no!" intervened the owner; "I have lost a law suit with Noël Beaudoin of St. Henri: I won't name my canoe *Noël!*"

"In that case we might call her the *Infant-Jesus*," proposed one of the crew.

"Tanfan Rhéaume, you'd better hold your tongue. We are not at church here. Would you only promise never to swear on board this canoe, if it was called the *Infant-Jesus?*"

"Well . . . now . . ."

"Of course not, you wouldn't. We are too great sinners, do you hear me? all of us, to give such names to our canoes."

"If we called her *Santa Claus* . . ." said a voice.

"Yes! to have her rush with her load into Mother Begin's garret, like Michel Couture's canoe which bore that name? You remember when she broke her rope running down the Fraser hill?"

"Into a garret, you said?"

"Yes, Madame, at night, on her way down

The Phantom Head

from St. Joseph, by land. The road turns there, and as the roof end of the house is on the same level as the hill, the canoe, which was laden with an ox, broke loose, and instead of following the curve, rushed madly into the house, right through the walls, knocking over everything on her passage, stoves, partition frames and bedstead with their contents. You can imagine. . . . Michel Couture had to pay one hundred dollars for that."

"And she was called *Santa Claus*?"

"The canoe? Yes, Madame."

"Was it also on Christmas Eve?" asked the lady with a smile.

"Oh! no!" was the laughing answer; "that would have been too much."

"Listen to me; I fancy my proposal will be agreed upon," said I, advancing towards the group. "Let us give our canoe the name of her godmother, by Jove! What is your christian name, Madam?"

"Mary, sir."

"Bravo, that's it, Merry Christmas!" cried out old Baron, unknowingly hazarding an English pun for the first time in his life.

Christmas in French Canada

"Merry Christmas! hurrah!..."

At this moment, the first call to midnight mass rang in the distance, and at the majestic sound of the bells of Notre-Dame in full peal, the traditional libation glided over the prow of the swift canoe, while twenty joyful voices cried: "Merry Christmas!" to the echoes of the lofty hills which face the rock of old Quebec.

A few minutes later, my companions and I were warmly nestled down amid the heavy furs heaped at the bottom of the canoe. The light craft, with her prow turned towards the river, advanced slowly at first, head overhanging in the space, balanced there for one moment, and then, carried away by the weight of the paddlers jumping aboard, she shot forward like an arrow, dived into the waves, rebounded like a ball, and under the effort of eight good paddles skilfully handled, swept off in the whirling foam.

"Merry Christmas!" cried the paddlers.

"Merry Christmas!" repeated old Baron, who sat astern, bent on his long paddle wriggling in the eddy like the tail of a Triton.

The Phantom Head

"Let us have a song!" cried somebody.

"No, boys, no songs to-night!" said old Baron, "but a Christmas hymn if you like."

And with a true and sonorous voice which old age had not yet affected, the old veteran of the St. Lawrence canoe-men, intoned over our heads the old carol whose cheerful rhythm keeps time so well with the movement of the paddles, and which sums up the whole Christian Legend:

Il est né, le divin Enfant:
Jouez, hautbois! résonnez, musettes!
Il est né, le divin Enfant:
Chantons tous son avènement!

Christmas in French Canada

To which the manly voices of the crew answered in unison:

Il est né, le divin Enfant!

I shall never forget that wonderful voyage.

We sped on, rapidly, under the sparkling blue sky, flooded by the white rays of the moon, which spread afar its silvery glitter over the undulation of the waves. One could fancy that each star, as a magic spark, lighted thousands of flaming cressets here and there among the masses of the resting floes.

No, I shall never forget that delightful voyage.

Suddenly our way was barred by a vast piece of ice, flat-surfaced like a marble floor. In two seconds, our canoe was hauled on it; and we halted to contemplate the scene. It was fairy-like.

The steep shores of the St. Lawrence unrolled right and left their snowy tapering heights, which the roofs, the trees, the campaniles and the church steeples seemed to

The Phantom Head

perforate with dim or luminous points, like a fringe of silver embroidery.

Around us, on the breast of the gigantic river, as far as the eye could reach, white surfaces appeared in a soft diffused light, broken here and there by furrows, rents, crevices, pools, lakes of deep water, all spangled with reflections intensifying its inky darkness.

And all this in an atmosphere of biting cold, but the strange calmness of which penetrated the soul with an extraordinary impression of serenity.

For some time the church bells of Quebec had been mingling their clangor with the resounding peals from the other shore. Unconsciously overwhelmed by the grandeur of the spectacle, we instinctively pressed against each other, listening to the solemn voices of the sacred bronzes exchanging from height to height their call to prayer, through that wondrous night—sublime anniversary of the great event.

"Ave Maria!" cried out old Baron, taking off his heavy fur cap.

Christmas in French Canada

And all the sturdy canoe-men uncovered their heads, while their tawny faces glowed under the starry splendors of the night.

Impossible to picture the majesty of the scene!

"Nothing could be more beautiful!" exclaimed, with one voice, my two friends from Florida.

"And thank God, we have not seen the Phantom Head," uttered Nazaire Jodoin, setting his foot on the batture of Quebec.

. .   ,   .

Several years later, passing along the foot of the cliff which overhangs the cove where, like a bee-hive, hums the great ship-yard, I noticed the remains of an old canoe, on the shattered bow of which a tattered piece of tin bore the four letters "TMAS," half washed out by time and weather.

Was it the skeleton of the old *Merry Christmas* ?

OVISE

A FEW years ago, some peculiar circumstances had led to Nicolet —a pleasant little town situated on the banks of the Nicolet river—a family of five persons, neither rich nor poor, of neither humble nor brilliant condition, but in whose home the angel of happiness had always had

Christmas in French Canada

his corner at the hearth and his place at the table.

At the time of my story, the youngest of the three children—a delicate fair-haired little maid, with dark eyes—was just four years old; but her pretty face and her winning ways had already made her friends with the whole neighborhood.

Most of the time she spoke of herself in the third person, and this peculiarity contributed to make her name of Louise—which she pronounced *Ouise*—familiar to every one, from old Boivert's ferry to the Bishop's Palace.

When she leaned over the railing of the balcony, or when, light as a lark, she wandered in the alleys of the garden, her provoking little head emerging here and there among the rose bushes and honeysuckles, the old priests who passed by on their way to the Bishop's, the students who turned the corner of the college avenue, the gentlemen and the ladies who followed the sidewalk of the main street, never failed to say:

"*Bonjour, Louise!*"

Ouise

To which a fresh and laughing baby voice invariably answered:

"*Bonzour!*"

The carters and the lumbermen who returned from the sawmills after their day's work, smiled to her with a pleasant word:

"*Bonsoir, mamzelle Louise!*"

And the little one answered in her clear ringing voice, like a bird's call:

"*Bonsoir, monsieur!*"

Often she stopped the coachmen with a sign of her dimpled finger, and when they came nearer to ask what she wanted:

"A drive!" she whispered, with a whole regiment of lurking smiles nestled at the corners of her eyes and mouth.

Sometimes they would object:

"I am in a hurry, Mamzelle Louise."

But then, she would put the index of her right hand on the index of her left, and with an accent of irresistible coaxing:

"A lit. . . lit. . . little one!" she would pray, varying her gentle intonations in the most exquisite manner.

That was all; the coachman would stop,

Christmas in French Canada

look at her a moment, and then yielding to a fit of surly kindness, would grumble:

"What a child! Impossible to refuse her anything."

And seizing the little one in his two sturdy hands, he would place her on the seat of his vehicle, jump to her side, give a crack of his whip, and start at random, while the child shook her fair curls in the wind, and her peals of laughter rang in the ears of the passers-by, who looked at her with a smile.

In short, Louise was a favorite.

Did she love anyone in return?

Did she love anyone? Why, she loved everybody. Oh, yes! But, after her father, mother, brother and sister, the one she loved the best was her dog.

For Mademoiselle Louise had a dog, a fine French *griffon*, very queer in his heavy fleece, which completely covered his eyes, a good doggy who had been named *Corbeau*, on account of his being a jet black. And, on his part, the dog had taken a fancy to the child, and never left her the breadth of

Ouise

his sole, if this expression be permitted when talking of dogs.

If one thing more than another had the power to throw Louise into fits of mirth, it was that old popular ballad, which her father used to sing to her, and which began thus:

> *Il était un petit homme*
> *Qui s'appelait Guilleri,*
> *Carabi!*
> *Il s'en fut à la chasse,*
> *A la chasse aux perdrix,*
> *Titi, carabi! Toto, carabo!*

"Toto Corbeau!" exclaimed the little one.

And her ringing laughter sparkled like a piece of fireworks.

The first time she was taken to confession, her father said to her:

"You will pray for me, won't you, Louise."

"Oh! yes, papa!" she answered.

And when, on her return, she was asked if she had remembered her promise:

"Yes, papa," she said, "Ouise told two big sins for you; there!"

As the winter feasts drew near, the papa had gone to Montreal for a short trip. He

Christmas in French Canada

returned home on the very day before Christmas, with a small, but rather heavy trunk he could not open, having, to the great disappointment of the little ones, unfortunately lost the key on his way.

Of the contents of the mysterious trunk, he had not the slightest recollection.

At all events, it could not be Christmas presents, as, for one reason or another, he had found all the stores of Montreal closed. And, what was even more annoying, he had been short of money.

Under such conditions, how could he have purchased anything at all? It was very disappointing indeed; but everyone knows that on Christmas Eve Santa Claus makes his round with his basket full of presents for good children.

"Well, now, my honeys," said the father, "put your shoes in the fire-place, hang up your stockings at the foot of your beds, say your prayers, and—quick, under the blankets! To-morrow morning we shall see what the little ones' friend will have brought to you. If you sleep well, you may be sure that he won't forget you."

Ouise

The boy—full credit must be given to him for that—had a kind of smile which denoted a certain air of incredulity; the eldest sister remained somewhat pensive; but Louise began to dance, clapping her hands, uttering bursts of laughter and loud ringing cries of joy.

Suddenly she stopped, and had a moment of serious thought. Then, lifting up her inquisitive eyes, she said to her father:

"Will Santa Claus also bring something to the little Jesus in the church?"

"No, my child."

"Why not?"

"Because the little Jesus needs nothing; all things belong to him."

"Yes, papa, he needs something; he is poor; Ouise saw him to-day. He has no clothes; he must feel cold, cold. The poor baby will cry."

And the little one, almost moved to tears put her finger to her trembling lips, her breast quivering like that of a bird seized by a feather of its wing.

But childish emotions pass quickly; the

Christmas in French Canada

good-night parting and the preparation for rest made a happy diversion.

Three good sounding kisses to papa, three tender hugs to mamma, and ten minutes later, three pairs of fine new shoes lay on the stones of the hearth, and three gentle heads, fair and dark, sank into three white pillows, in the shadow of the curtains caressed by the trembling glimmers of the night lamp.

As one may guess, the key of the trunk was easily found. And presents of all kinds soon crammed the shoes in the fireplace; a big doll gorgeously dressed was laid across those of Louise; the little stockings hanging at the foot of the beds were filled up with candies and pretty gifts by the discreet hand of the mamma; and when, before retiring, the papa threw a loving glance through the half-opened door behind which rested his treasures, he fancied he could see a swarm of those winged spirits called dreams fluttering around the brow of his darling pet, murmuring to her ears some of the divine secrets which, that night especially, the angels of Heaven exchange between

Ouise

themselves in the enchantments of their eternal felicity.

And while the servants passed the threshold on tip-toe to attend the midnight mass, the father and mother, kept at home by paternal duty, went to sleep, lulled by the solemn chimes of the bells chanting their aerial hymns through the night.

At the first gleaming of the day, both were wakened up by joyful exclamations.

An uproar of trumpets, of drums and fiddles, broken by silvery voices, came up from the lower storey.

In two minutes the house was on foot, gathered in one group.

"But where is the other one?" asked the father, kissing the two eldest children. "Is not Louise up yet?"

"She is," said the mother; "her bed is empty."

"Where is she, then?"

"Don't know," answered the little ones.

"Louise!"

"Louise!"

Rather puzzled, all hands began a search.

Christmas in French Canada

"Where is the dog?" asked the father anxiously.

"Corbeau!"

"Corbeau!"

"Corbeau!"

No answer, not even a growl.

The poor father gave a cry of alarm:

"The dog is not here! the child is gone! Good Heavens, where is she?"

And almost crazy, he rushed out bareheaded, without even noticing that the door bolt was drawn.

A thin coat of snow had fallen during the night; footprints were visible crossing the front garden and leading towards the cathedral. One could easily detect the tracks of two little feet together with that kind of rosette, in the shape of a five-leafed clover, which the foot of a dog imprints.

This somewhat reassured the anxious father, who continued his run in the direction indicated by the traces.

He had not gone a hundred paces when he stood face to face with the Bishop, an old college companion, who came to him holding

"*I bring you back a little saint*"

Page 178

by the right hand the little maid, whose left disappeared among the long and shaggy hairs of the *griffon*.

"I bring back to you a little saint," said the Bishop.

And handing to his friend a small parcel he held under his arm:

"With a restitution," added he, smiling.

The father was soon acquainted with what had happened.

It was dark yet, and the lamps, lighted since five o'clock at the Bishop's Palace, had not yet yielded before the morning dawn when the door bell was heard.

It was old Thérèse, the gardener, who answered the call.

A type worth picturing, this same Thérèse.

Imagine an old crone, who worked hard, grumbling from morning till night, smoked like a locomotive, and who, satisfied or dissatisfied, had only one energetic expression to show forth her joy or discontent: "*Cré million!*"

If you gave her a few cents, some tobacco,

Christmas in French Canada

some old clothes, or even a glass of wine, she never failed to say:

"Thank you, cré million! that's exactly what's good for me."

If the little brats of the neighbourhood entered her garden, walked on her flower-beds or plundered her rose-bushes:

"Cré million!" she said: "hold on a bit, you scoundrels; I'll hang you by the ears on the handle of the door."

The children, who knew the value of her threats, were not frightened more than was necessary—and had given her the surname of *Million*, to which she seemed to have no objection.

It was she who went to the door.

"*Bonzour, Miyon!*" said a little voice from out the dark.

Thérèse drew near: it was Louise with her dog and a little parcel she held with outstretched arms as something precious and sacred.

"Why, is it you, *puceron?*" cried the old maid; "what are you about at such an hour?"

Ouise

" Want to see *Monsieur Monseigneur.*"

" Monseigneur! Monseigneur! Cré million! he has something better to do than listen to your nonsense, Monseigneur. Come in and warm yourself. Did you ever see the like?"

" What is it?" asked a low paternal voice, well known to the little girl.

And the good Bishop appeared in the opening of the ante-chamber.

" What is it?"

" It's me."

" Who you?"

" Ouise!"

" Louise! upon my word! so it is. Who is with you?"

"Corbeau."

" Does your father know?"

" Is asleep."

"And what are you here for?"

" Ouise brings a dress for the little Jesus."

" You bring a dress for the little Jesus?"

" Yes; Ouise saw him yesterday; has no dress. Feels cold, cold."

" But where did you get that dress?"

And the child told, in her baby language

Christmas in French Canada

with hesitation and stammering efforts at the long words, how she had put her shoes in the fire-place before going to bed; how Santa Claus had come during the night and brought her a big doll with a nice new dress; how she had then thought of the Infant-Jesus all alone in his manger in the big cold church; and, at last, how she had taken off the doll's dress to bring it to the poor little Jesus.

The Bishop listened with emotion.

"But now your doll is going to be cold too," said he.

"Oh! no, she's wrapped up in Ouise's shawl."

"Well, then, come away!" said the good prelate, stealthily passing the end of his finger in the corner of his eye, "I shall take you back to your papa; you will dress up your doll again; and, as to the little Jesus, don't be anxious about him, I shall have his manger warmed so that he will be quite comfortable."

"Surely?"

"Surely! You will see to it, won't you, Thérèse?"

Thérèse was wiping her eyes with the corner of her apron.

Ouise

"Cré million! my lord," she said, "I'm ready to heat him until he melts."

"All right, then; and now, Louise, here is a nice picture for you; it is the picture of the little Jesus himself."

"Thank you, Monsieur Monseigneur."

"You like it?"

"Oh! yes; have you got another one?"

"You want two? what for?"

"Ouise wants one for her Indian."

"What Indian?"

"Godd Indian brought Ouise to mamma, when Ouise lit— lit— little."

The Bishop and old Thérèse had a good laugh, and the Indian was made happy too.*

It is a received tradition with our little ones that they are brought to their parents by a "good Indian," which theory is at least as effective as that of the Cabbage Leaf.

THE HORSESHOE.

THE narrator was a well-known Montrealer.

I was spending the winter in New Orleans, said he, in company with a countryman of ours, whom I shall call Alphonse, if you permit me: the most amiable of comrades, the most loyal of friends, but at the same time the greatest fatalist in Creation.

So complete a fatalist that, one day, in the open street, he almost fell into my arms, exclaiming joyfully:

"My dear fellow, congratulate me: I have just lost a five dollar bill."

And before I had time to remark that I failed to see in this any serious subject of

The Horseshoe

felicitation, he was executing a mazurka step on the sidewalk to the great amazement of the passers-by.

That morning he had accidentally broken a small looking glass, and he expected all kinds of dreadful casualities in the course of the day. The loss of the five dollars had averted the threatening fatality; hence the exuberance of his joy.

A black cat, in particular, had the effect of exasperating him to madness. He would have walked miles to avoid the sight of one.

It was the first winter I had ever passed in a southern climate; and knowing nothing in the shape of December temperature but the snow storms of Quebec and the freezing north winds of Chicago, I lived in ecstacy, literally intoxicated with sunshine and perfumed breezes.

As for my friend, he was a jolly fellow eagerly feasting upon the sweet fruit of heedless youth; and, free from all annoyances, anxieties and regrets of any kind, we led together the merriest bachelor life that could be dreamed of.

Christmas in French Canada

Our mornings were devoted to work; but the afternoons . . . . but the evenings . . . . all left to our fancies!

Alphonse was connected with a large firm, exporters of Louisiana produce; and on the same floor as the offices, but in rear, and separated from them by a large and almost empty hall, which served occasionally as a store room for samples, he had fitted up a very pretty suite of apartments which we shared like two brothers.

The partition walls which separated us from the offices were glass-framed from the dado to the ceiling; so that from our bedroom—it was this apartment especially that we amicably shared—we could see more or less what was going on in the front rooms, through which was our only exit.

A narrow ante-chamber put us in communication with the wareroom.

Christmas drew near . . . . New Year's also, naturally; and we looked forward to all sorts of good times, of joyous parties with pleasant acquaintances.

One evening, however, on returning home

The Horseshoe

after a night passed at a planter's of the neighborhood, I found Alphonse in a most gloomy mood.

A dark colored cat, according to his story, had entered our rooms, that morning; and John, our old servant, who was, by the way, nearly as dark as the intruder, aided by all available hands, had succeeded in ridding the house of this new guest, but only after endless difficulties.

For two long days, my friend seemed worried and strangely preoccupied.

This brilliant talker, always ready for a hearty laugh, was turning taciturn.

The black cat might have annoyed him, no doubt; but to have disturbed him to such an extent was beyond all reasonable supposition.

"Look here," said I, on Christmas Eve, while he was searching every corner of the room in a nervous and impatient manner, "what is the matter with you, anyhow?"

"The matter with me," said he, in a furious tone, "the matter with me is that I have been robbed,—that's all!"

Christmas in French Canada

"Robbed!"

"Yes, robbed! and the worst of it is," added he, letting his arms fall in dejection, "the worst of it is that I am afraid to suspect...."

"Whom do you mean?"

"I mean John. Do you understand? To suspect some one hitherto considered honest. Discharging a poor fellow, dishonouring an old servant, with the risk of punishing an innocent man.... I wouldn't do that for ten times what I have lost. And still...."

"But what is it you have lost?"

"My pocket-book."

"With money in it?"

"With two bills of five hundred each."

"No!"

"Yes, my friend; I had drawn that money from the bank to conclude a bargain, in the evening, with an old Creole. You know that most of those old Creoles won't hear of checks; scarcely will they accept green-backs. Now, the man having missed his appointment, the two bills remained in my pocket-book. It was there, in the inside

The Horseshoe

pocket of my waistcoat on the back of that chair, when I turned in the night before last; and now it is gone. Oh! that cursed black cat!"

"And you have searched everywhere for it?"

"I have turned everything inside out... But, no more of this," he added, seizing me by the arm and turning my head towards the little fancy stove which stood in the centre of our bedroom; "it shall be the last time such a stupid thing will happen to me."

"What is that?"

"A horseshoe, which I have just found on the street. I can defy bad luck now."

And sure enough, I saw the gleam of a half-worn and polished horseshoe balanced on the central ornament of the little heater.

"And you believe...?" said I with a smile.

"Yes, I believe!" he interrupted with conviction. "You shall see for yourself."

"Well, then, let us get to dinner; we shall drink the health of the wizard who is to bring back the star of good luck to our

Christmas in French Canada

horizon. If he only could bring back your pocket-book!"

"Who knows? At all events, let us dine; we shall sup after midnight mass. I have ordered some good *croquignoles* at Victor's to remind us of our home."

"A good idea! but is midnight mass of great importance to you?"

"Of course. The artists of the Opera are going to sing at the Jesuits', you know."

"Then you shall go alone, for I have an appointment for high mass to-morrow."

"And what about the *croquignoles?*"

"You'll take some home with you, that's all."

And thus it happened that on the 25th of December, 1870, by one o'clock in the morning, I was sleeping alone—our servant having his lodging elsewhere—in our bachelor quarters of Poydras street, in the city of New Orleans, while, under the illuminated vaults of the churches, resounded the joyful carols of that mysterious Christmas night so dear to all Christian hearts.

Suddenly, I awoke.

The Horseshoe

A noise was heard in the direction of the offices.

"Here is Alphonse coming in," said I to myself; "I should have left the gas lighted."

Now, for some weeks past, a strange excitement had reigned in New Orleans.

People talked of nothing else but burglars and burglaries.

Every morning, the newspapers contained accounts of broken doors, of forced drawers, of plundered safes.

The police were of no avail. The bold thieves set watchmen and detectives at defiance with extraordinary skill and unheard of audacity.

While they were apparently cornered at one point, they operated in another direction, and generally with successful result.

The plundering of iron safes was their principal specialty, and when the same resisted picklocks and other instruments, they used gun-cotton, nitro-glycerine or any other kind of explosive to break open hinges and safety locks.

In short, the city was constantly upon the alert.

Christmas in French Canada

Now, to return to my narrative: at the very moment when I was making the remark that I ought to have left the gas lighted to guide my companion, I perceived, on turning my head, a faint and intermittent reflection playing on the glass partition of our room.

"So much the better," thought I; "he has a light."

I waited.

No footsteps—complete silence.

"What is he about?" I muttered, kneeling on my bed to look in the direction of the offices.

"Why, he is not alone!" said I, somewhat surprised; "and what has he got to do at the cashier's office?"

At the same moment, the light of a dark lantern flashed across my face, and I saw two shadows bending over one of the safes of the establishment; I even heard the clicking of the safety knob.

A thought, rapid as a flash of lightning, made me shiver from head to foot.

No doubt, they were burglars.

What was going to happen?

The Horseshoe

Would the thieves be satisfied with the plundering of the offices?

Would they venture in my direction?

And then . . . .

How to escape? how to give an alarm? how defend myself? I was in a closed trap, without a weapon, without even a stick.

I was even unable to dress, for fear the slightest noise might attract the attention of the ruffians, and reveal my presence.

On the other hand, it was folly to stay in bed.

A thought came to me: the horseshoe!

And here I am creeping out of my sheets as cautiously as possible; and stealthily, quietly, slowly, I made my way towards the stove where I saw, glittering vaguely in the pale light of the night, the only weapon a mere hazard had left to my disposal.

A moment later I stood in the antechamber, half hidden behind the frame of the door opening on the back store, in night gown, with chattering teeth and shaking limbs, holding my breath, the perspiration of anguish on my forehead, a desperate

Christmas in French Canada

pang in my heart, and the horseshoe in my hand.

One is generally more timid abroad than at home. Besides, to be started from sleep as I had been, is not calculated to give confidence. I was terribly afraid.

Did the waiting last long? I cannot say; but it seemed an age to me.

Of what the thieves had done in the meanwhile, I had no idea. I had lost my head, and I waited for the end, with only one hope: that the burglars, satisfied with their plunder, would start off without discovering me.

That hope was vain.

The two shadows which seemed monstrously tall, left the offices and were coming straight toward me, the light of the lanterns wandering right and left as if to explore the premises, and at last falling right on the open door, where, dumb with terror, and more dead than alive, I expected the catastrophe which surely could not fail to be near at hand.

At this critical moment, the courage of despair sprang up in my heart, and I recovered my coolness for one instant.

The Horseshoe

I considered the situation.

I said to myself that there was only one chance of escape left to me: not to wait the assault but to fell one of the enemy by a first blow, and then go for the other, man to man.

Not a second elapsed between the thought and its execution.

The two men advanced almost entirely lost in the dark, their reflectors projecting two cones of light right before them.

It was then that I suddenly appeared, as white as a ghost in the lighted opening of the door; and rapid as a thunderbolt, uttering a wild cry of rage, I shot out my weapon with all my strength and with terrible precision, right at the head of one of the supposed bandits.

Clic! . . . . a sharp and metallic sound was heard, together with a formidable voice yelling:

"Damn it! don't kill the police!"

The reaction made me stagger; it was so sudden that I could hardly stammer a word of excuse to the poor guardian of the

Christmas in French Canada

peace whose death I was so nearly having on my conscience.

All was explained.

Leaving for the midnight mass, Alphonse had inadvertently left the big iron door which led to our apartments unclosed; the spring lock had not caught.

The two policemen, particularly on the lookout for signs of burglary, had, on their night watch, pushed the door, and finding it unlocked, entered the house in search of possible mischief.

They had visited the offices, examined the iron safes, and were just completing their inspection by a tour about the other parts of the building, when my weapon had struck and broken the brass number which shone on the front of my man's shako.

If the blow had struck two inches lower, the unfortunate man would have been killed.

I recovered by degrees, and when my friend Alphonse returned from church puzzled to see the door open, he found me busy uncorking a bottle of old Kentucky Bourbon, to restore my nerves in the first place, and

The Horseshoe

then to drink the health of my would-be burglars, two good Irish fellows who laughed at my frenzy with mouths split open to the ears.

"Here's to your luck!" they exclaimed with the most enthusiastic spirit.

"Here's to your luck, old friends!" answered I with no less undisguised satisfaction.

"Merry Christmas!" intervened Alphonse coming in; "here are the *croquignoles!*"

"Merry Christmas and a happy New Year!"

"God bless ye all, and Erin go bragh!"

My comrade was soon acquainted with the situation.

"You see, old fellow," he said to me, "that it is good sometimes to have a horseshoe near one's hand."

"It is better anyhow than to have it in the face," said the policeman who had so narrowly escaped my blow.

"By the way," I remarked, "speaking of the horseshoe, what has become of it?"

"I don't know," said one of the patrol men.

Christmas in French Canada

"Neither do I," said the other.

"The fact is, I did not hear it fall," said I.

"Let us look for it."

And armed with candles and with the two lanterns, we began to search for the horseshoe in every possible corner of the place.

"But where could it be?"

"It cannot be very far, anyway."

"To get out of the room, it should have passed through the glass partition."

"And we heard no sound whatever."

"And not a pane broken."

"Strange, isn't it?"

"Unless it be on the top of that. . . " ventured one of the policemen.

And he pointed out a pile of empty barrels standing endwise in one corner of the store, and which almost reached the ceiling.

"It is impossible!"

"Well, I shall judge for myself," said Pat. "Lend me your shoulders, Michael."

And Pat climbed the pile of old barrels, which resounded joyfully under the

The Horseshoe

pressure and hammering of his hands and knees.

At last he reached the summit.

"Hurrah, boys!" cried he, "here's the beggar!"

And he triumphantly brandished the horseshoe.

Suddenly:

"Hold on!" said he; "there's something else. What's this? A pocket-book, by Jove!"

"My pocket-book!" exclaimed Alphonse.

And the brave policeman almost fell into our arms, with the pocket-book in his hand.

"It wouldn't have remained there twenty years," said he. "Good hiding place. Pretty smart, the thief."

Alphonse was hugging me, laughing to tears.

"Friend, friend," said he, "the horseshoe! will you believe in it now?"

But after a while his face took an expression of sadness, and he threw the pocket-book on his bed.

Christmas in French Canada

"Oh! John," said he, with a gesture of discouragement, "I would have risked a fortune in his hands. Who can be trusted now?"

In the morning, John made his appearance, and between us three, we found the key to the enigma.

From the waistcoat hanging on the back of the chair, the pocket-book had dropped into a boot which had happened to lie right underneath.

The infernal black cat, chased by all the broom-sticks of the establishment, had taken refuge on the pile of whisky barrels. The boot, thrown by Alphonse's supple wrist, had turned out the animal, but had fallen back empty.

The pocket-book had remained on the top of the pile of barrels; and, as nobody would ever have suspected its presence in such a place, it might, in spite of Pat's opinion, have stayed there twenty years and more, had it not been for the horse-shoe.

As for good old John, if he is still living,

The Horseshoe

he doubtless remembers the Christmas box he took home that evening.

And as for me, I never thought one could be so terribly scared on a Christmas Eve.

TOM. CARIBOO.

"CRIC, *crac*, girls and boys! *Parlons, parlee, parlow!* The whole thing if you want to know, pass the spittoon to Fiddle Joe; *sacatabi, sac-à-tabac*, all who are deaf will please draw back."

It is hardly necessary to mention that the narrator who thus commenced his speech was Fiddle Joe himself, my friend Fiddle Joe, presiding over a *veillée de contes* (a story telling party), on Christmas Eve, at the blacksmith's, old Jean Bilodeau.

Tom Cariboo

Poor old Bilodeau, it is over fifty years now since I heard the sound of his anvil, and I fancy I can see him yet, sitting in the light, with his elbows on his knees, and the shank of his short pipe tightly held between his three remaining teeth.

Fiddle Joe was a queer kind of a fellow, very interesting and very popular, who had spent his youth in the shanties, and was very fond of relating his travelling adventures in the *pays d'en haut*, the timber lands of the Ottawa, the Gatineau and the St. Maurice.

That day he happened to have a fit of inspiration.

He had been *compère* in the morning, which meant he had stood as godfather to a new-born child; and, as the accessories of the ceremony had brought a slight breeze into the sails of his natural eloquence, his stories went on marvellously.

All camp and forest incidents of course: fights, casualties, fishings extraordinary, miraculous hunting exploits, visions, sorcery, feats of all kinds; he had a collection to suit every taste.

Christmas in French Canada

"Do tell us a Christmas story, Joe, if you know one, to fill up time until we leave for church," cried a girl by the name of Phémie Boisvert.

And Fiddle Joe, who prided himself on knowing what was due to the fair sex, had responded by the characteristic formula as above. Then, after having moistened his throat with a finger deep of Jamaica, and lighted his pipe at the candle, with one of those long cedar splinters which were used by our country folk before, and even after the invention of phosphorus matches, he opened his narrative in the following terms:

This is to tell you, my friends, that, on that year, we had gone rafting above Bytown, at the elbow of a small river called La Galeuse, a funny name but which is of no importance to what I am going to relate.

We were fifteen in our camp: beginning with the boss, and ending with the choreboy.

Nearly all were good men, not quarrelsome, not given to cuss words—of course I don't speak of a little innocent swearing here and there to keep things going—and not drunk

Tom Cariboo

ards—with the exception of one, I must acknowledge—a tough one indeed.

As for this fellow, boys, he was not exactly what may be called a drunkard: when he happened to come face to face with a demijohn, or when his lips met those of flask or bottle, he was no longer a man, he was a regular funnel.

He came somewhere back of Three Rivers.

His real name was Thomas Baribeau; but as our foreman, who was Irish, had always some difficulty over this French name, we had nicknamed him "TOM CARIBOO."

Thomas Baribeau—Tom Cariboo—it sounded pretty much the same, as you see. At all events, it was the fellow's *nom de guerre*, and the boss had caught it as easily as though it had been a name freshly imported from Cork.

Anyhow, to speak in polite terms, Tom Cariboo, or Thomas Baribeau, as you wish, had a galvanized-iron throat of the first quality, and he was, moreover, a patented ruffian; but something out of the common, to give the Devil his due.

When I think of all I have heard him say

Christmas in French Canada

against God, the Blessed Virgin, the good angels, the saints of Heaven and all the Holy Trinity taken together, I still feel a shiver down my back.

Oh! the worthless swagger, what a scamp he was!

He swore, he lied, he cursed his father and mother five or six times a day, he never said a word of prayer; in short, I don't hesitate to say that his miserable carcase, with his soul into the bargain, was not worth, with due respect to the company, the wag of a dog's tail. That's my opinion.

There were not a few in our crowd who swore to having seen him on four paws, at night, in the fields, roving about in the shape of some devilish *loup-garou*.

As for me, my friends, I saw the brute on all fours several times, but, take my word, he was neither playing the *loup-garou*, nor anything so respectable, I assure you: he was too beastly drunk for that.

Anyhow, I must tell you that, for some time, I was one of those who thought if the rascal practised any sorcery at all, he had a

Tom Cariboo

preference for the *chasse-galerie*; for, one night, Titoine Pelchat, one of our road cutters, had spied him coming down a big tree, when the pagan had told him: "Toine, curse my soul! if you ever mention a word of this to anybody, I'll rip you cold, that's all!"

Of course, Titoine had not failed to tell everybody in the shanty, but in the greatest confidence.

If you don't know what the *chasse-galerie* is, my friends, I am the man to post you fine on the matter, for the *chasse-galerie* I can boast of having seen with my own eyes.

Yes, I, Fiddle Joe, one Sunday afternoon, 'twixt mass and vespers, in full daylight, I saw the infernal machine pass in the air, right in front of the church of St. Jean Deschaillons, on my soul and conscience, as clear as I see you now.

It was something like a canoe, which travelled, rapidly as an arrow, at about five hundred feet above the earth, manned by a dozen reprobates in red flannel shirts, paddling like damnation, with Satan standing in the

Christmas in French Canada

stern, steering straight forward in the direction of Three Rivers.

We could even hear them sing in chorus with all sorts of devilish voices:

l"la l'bon vent! v'là l'joli vent!*

But I may say there are many who don t require such a display to practise *chasse-galerie*.

The regular scalawags like Tom Cariboo, have only to climb up a tree, and launch themselves on a branch, or stick, or anything else, and the Devil drives them on.

Thus they travel thousands of miles in a single night to concoct God knows what kind of jugglery, in some infernal recess where honest people wouldn't set foot for a fortune.

---

*The origin of this *chasse-galerie* legend can be traced to the middle ages. In France and Germany, they had what was called the Black Huntsman. It was a fantastic coursing which rode in the air with wild clamour and desperate speed, through the darkness of the night. In French Canada, by a curious phenomena of mirage observed in some circumstance similar to that related by Fiddle Joe, a mounted canoe was seen flying through the air, and the same was naturally substituted for the Black Huntsman, who went also, in some Province of France, by the name of *Chasse-galerie*. It was supposed that the lumbermen—who, by the way, did not enjoy a very enviable reputation—managed through some devilish process, to travel in this way to save fatigue and shorten the distance.

Tom Cariboo

At all events, if Tom Cariboo did not practise *chasse-galerie*, when he used to steal out alone at night, peeping about to see if anybody watched him, it was certainly not to go to confession, for, to the astonishment of our gang, although there was not a drop of liquor in the whole shanty, the blackguard smelt, every morning, like an old whiskey-cask.

Where did he get the stuff?

It was in the latter part of December, and Christmas was drawing near, when another gang working for the same firm, about fifteen miles higher up on the Galeuse, sent word that if we wanted to attend midnight mass, we had only to join them, for a missionary on his way down from the Nipissing would be there to celebrate it.

"By Jove!" we said, "it is seldom enough that we see an Infant-Jesus in the shanties, let us go!"

We are not angels in the lumber camps, you know that, boys. Even when we don't plague all the saints in the calendar and scandalize the *Bon Dieu* from morning till

Christmas in French Canada

night like Tom Cariboo, one can't reasonably pass six months in the woods and six months on the rafts every year, without getting a little "off" on his duties.

But there must be a limit to rascality. Although one may not wear out his knees in the church, or play *mistigri* every night with the beadle, he likes to remember at times, do you see, that a good Canadian boy has something else than the soul of a dog in the mould of his waistcoat, so to speak.

Consequently the trip was soon decided upon, and everything carefully stowed for the occasion.

It was brilliant moonlight; the snow was fine for a tramp; we could start after supper, be there in time for mass, and back again for breakfast in the morning, in case we could not spend the night over there.

'You shall go by yourselves, you confounded fools!" cried Tom Cariboo, with a string of blasphemies, almost splitting his knuckles with a blow of his fist on the shanty table.

As you may well imagine, none of us

Tom Cariboo

thought of kneeling down to coax the ruffian. The absence of such a parishioner could not spoil the ceremony, and there was no need of his sweet breathing voice to intone the sacred hymns.

"Well, if you don't wish to go," said the foreman, "do as you please, my dear fellow. You'll stay here to watch the fire. And since you don't care about seeing God, I hope you won't see the Devil, while we are away."

Well then, boys, off we go, with belts tight around the waists, snow shoes well fastened at the toes of our moccasins, each with his little bag of eatables on his shoulder, and a twist of tobacco right behind his teeth.

As we had only to follow the frozen bed of the river, the road was a trifle of course; and we marched on, singing "*La Boulangère*," on the fine, levelled, white snow, under a sky as transparent as crystal, without a crevice or jolting to hamper our progress.

All I can say, my friends, is that merry parties of that kind are far between in shanty life.

'Pon my word, I fancied we could hear

Christmas in French Canada

the old church bell pealing: "Come on! come on!" as in the good old times; and more than once, bless my soul! I couldn't help turning round and looking back to see if we were not followed by some of the fine little Canadian trotters of home, with manes floating in the wind, and a row of merry bells ringing at their martingales.

That's what sharpens the wit of a country boy, I tell you. And you ought to have seen Fiddle Joe paddling his canoe that night!

I suppose it is useless to tell you that our midnight mass was not as brilliant as an archbishop's ceremony.

The vestments of the priest were not exactly what may be called imposing; there was no danger of being blinded by the glare of the altar decoration; the singers' windpipes were not oiled like a nightingale's throat, and the acolytes would doubtless have showed a more natural gait with shoulder under a canthook than a censer at arm's length.

You may add, besides, that there wasn't

Tom Cariboo

even the shadow of an Infant-Jesus; which, as you all know, is no small drawback to a Christmas performance.

To tell the truth, the good old man Job himself couldn't have been more poorly fitted to say his daily mass.

But no matter, there are lots of church services with music and gilded ornaments which are not worth the one we had that night, my friends, take Fiddle Joe's word for it!

It reminded us of old times, do you see, of the old parish, of the old home, of the old mother, and all that.

Good gracious me! you all know that Fiddle Joe is no squinny nor crying baby; well, I had never done passing my quid from one cheek to the other to control my emotion.

But that's enough about this part; let us see what had happened to Tom Cariboo during our absence.

I need not tell you that, after the mass was over, we returned to our camp by the same way, so that it was full daylight when we reached the shanty.

At first, we were greatly surprised not to

Christmas in French Canada

see a single thread of smoke rising from the chimney; but we were still more astonished when we found the door wide open, the stove without an ember, and not a trace of Tom Cariboo.

As true as I live, our first thought was that the Devil had carried him away. A worthless chap like him, do you see. . .

But, after all, that was no reason for not looking for him.

Hard enough it was to look for him, for not a bit of snow had fallen for several days, and the consequence was there were thousands of foot-prints around the shanty and even in the surrounding woods, all so well crossed and mixed up together, that it was impossible to make out anything of them.

Fortunately the boss had a very smart dog: *Polisson*, as we used to call him for a pet name.

"Search, Polisson!" said we.

And off goes Polisson searching out right and left, his nose in the snow, wagging his tail, while the rest of us followed on with a double-barrelled gun loaded with bullets, and which I carried myself.

Tom Cariboo

A good gun in a shanty is like the petticoat of a woman in a family. Remember that, my friends.

We had not been two minutes peeping through the branches, when our dog suddenly stood still in his tracks, trembling like a leaf. 'Pon my word, if he had not been ashamed I think the scamp would have made a right about for the house.

As for me, I threw up my gun and stepped forward.

You'll never imagine, my friends, what I saw right in front of me, on the slope of a ravine where the wood was thicker and the snow heavier than elsewhere. . .

It wasn't funny at all, I tell you. Or rather, it would have been very funny, if it hadn't been so fearful.

Just fancy that our Tom Cariboo was roosted in the fork of a big wild cherry tree, pale as a winding-sheet, his eyes starting out of their sockets, at the muzzle of a she-bear who clung to the trunk about two feet below him.

Thunder! Fiddle Joe is not a man to

Christmas in French Canada

skedaddle when called upon to face a squall, you all know that; well, this terrible sight made my blood whirl up from my toes to the nape of my neck.

"This is the time not to miss your aim, my poor Fiddle Joe," said I to myself. "Point blank! or God save your soul!"

Shifting was no use: bing! bang! . . . I aimed and shot both barrels at once, my two bullets striking the beast right between the shoulders.

She gave a growl, stretched her paws, swung for a moment, and then fell headlong with her back broken.

It was high time. My gun was still smoking, when I saw another mass tumbling down from the tree.

It was Tom Cariboo, who spread himself fainting and sprawling right across the dying she-bear. He was terribly torn by her claws, which had struck him more than once, and his hair. . . Well, now, try and guess, my friends. . . His hair had all turned white!

Yes, as white as snow. Fear had turned his hair white in a single night, as true as

" After which it was the bear we had to drag to the camp"

Page 216

Tom Cariboo

I intend to take *un p'tit coup* by and by, with the grace of God, and the permission of Uncle Bilodeau, who shan't lose anything by it.

Yes, honestly, the rascal had suddenly grown so old, that some of us would not believe it was the same man.

We hurriedly made a kind of hand-barrow with branches, and we laid the poor fellow on it, cautiously handling that portion of his body which had been damaged by the bear's claws; and so carried him back to the shanty half dead, and frozen nearly as hard as a piece of Bologna sausage.

After which, it was the bear we had to drag to the camp.

But here's the fun of it.

You may call me a liar if you wish; it wasn't credible, but the infernal beast seemed to have inherited poor Tom's most characteristic quality, and was smelling of rum like a seasoned cask, so much so that Titoine Pelchat said it gave him a mind to lick the animal.

But it was no miracle.

Christmas in French Canada

You know, my friends — if you don't, Fiddle Joe will tell you — that the bears don't spend their winters working hard as we do, poor lumbermen building rafts for the spring.

So far are they from working, that they haven't even the energy to eat.

At the first frosts of Autumn, they dig a hole between the roots of a tree, and lie there for the winter, buried alive in the snow which the animal's breath melts from the inside, so as to form a kind of oven where they spend the whole season, half asleep like marmots, and licking their paws for a living.

Our own, that is Tom Cariboo's bear, had chosen the roots of that particular cherry tree to shelter himself, while Tom had chosen a forked branch in the same. . . You'll know what for in a moment.

Only, as you remember that the ground was on a slope, Tom Cariboo — which was quite natural — gained his branch from the upper side of the declivity; and the she-bear —which was natural also—had dug her hole

Tom Cariboo

from the lower side, where the roots were not so deeply buried in the sod.

This accounts for these two savages having lived neighbors and almost partners, without having ever met; each of them being under the impression that he had the exclusive possession of the premises for himself.

You will probably ask what business Tom Cariboo had in the fork of that tree.

Well, in that fork there was a hole, and in that hole our drunkard had hidden a jar of high-wines which he had smuggled into the camp, we never exactly knew how. I suppose he had made us tow it under water behind one of our canoes, at the end of a string.

At all events, he had it; and almost every night he would sneak out and climb the tree to fill his flask.

It was from that nest of his that Titoine Pelchat had seen him coming down, that time we spoke of the *chasse-galerie;* and that was why, every morning, one could have set the scoundrel on fire, merely by passing a live coal under his nose.

Christmas in French Canada

Well, then, after we had left for the midnight mass, Tom Cariboo had gone to fill his flask out of the hidden demijohn.

On a merry day like Christmas, of course, the flask was soon emptied, although there was only one drunkard to treat; and Tom returned to his cupboard to renew his stock.

Unfortunately, if the flask was empty, it was not the case with its master; on the contrary, its master was too full.

The demijohn, carelessly handled and uncorked, overflowed on the other side of the cherry tree, right on the muzzle of the she-bear.

At first, the animal had naturally licked her chops, sniffing; and then, finding that this kind of rain had a peculiar taste and smell, she had opened her eyes. Her eyes open, the whisky had flowed into them.

High-wines, friends! it's no use asking if the beast awoke for good.

On hearing her howls, Tom Cariboo began to descend the tree, but not a bit! Stop, boy! The bear, having also heard a noise,

Tom Cariboo

had walked around the tree, and before the poor devil was half way down, she had clapped a destroying paw on the most prominent part of the descending intruder.

But the monster was too torpid to do more; and, while our heathen was climbing back up the tree, bleeding and terrified, she remained clinging to the bark, without being able to follow further up.

That's what had happened. You see, that if the bear smelt of whisky, it was no miracle.

Tom Cariboo began to descend.

Poor Tom Cariboo! between ourselves, it

Christmas in French Canada

took three long weeks to repair his damages.

Never could we convince the repentant drunkard that it was not Satan who had appeared to him, and who had thus lacerated his. . . feelings.

You ought to have seen him, begging even the dog's pardon for all his oaths and all his nightly sprees.

He couldn't sit down, of course; and so had to kneel.

It was his punishment for having refused to do so on Christmas Eve.

And lifting his glass to his lips, Fiddle Joe added:

Cric, crac! . . Sacatabi sac-à-tabac! . . Here's to your luck, old Jack!

TITANGE

"THAT'S a rattling fine story!" said old Jean Bilodeau; "but haven't you got another one? There is plenty of time yet for midnight mass."

"Yes, tell us another story, Uncle Joe," said Phémie Boisvert; "don't

Christmas in French Canada

you know any about that *Chasse-galerie* you were speaking of just now?"

"Good!" said we all around, "a Christmas story of the *Chasse-Galerie*!"

Fiddle Joe had never to be asked twice:

"Very well," said he. "*Cric crac*, boys and girls . . . *Parlons, parlee, parlow* . . . "

Et cetera. And he went on:

This is to tell you, my friends, that, on that year, I was hired by old Dawson, for squaring timber at a lumber shanty he had opened at the entrance of the Rat River, on the St. Maurice, together with a gang of raftsmen from Three Rivers.

Although the *voyageurs* of Three Rivers are a pretty rough lot, as you will see by and by, the winter we spent there was peaceful enough, owing to a very extraordinary accident which happened to one of us on Christmas Eve, and which I am going to relate.

As you all know, I reckon, for squaring a piece of timber it requires two men, one to handle the squaring-axe, and the other to pick and butt; so the boss had mated me

Titange

with a queer fellow whom his comrades had nicknamed *Titange*.

Titange is a contraction for *petitange*, which means "little angel." A pretty odd name for a shantyman, but I couldn't help it, could I? What was the origin of that name?

"*Looked like a fritter out of the frying pan.*"

It appears the fellow had got it through his mother.

His father, Johnny Morissette, was as strongly built a man as could be found

Christmas in French Canada

among the St. Maurice voyageurs in his day, and although of a quiet character, was particularly proud of his muscles. Fancy how cheap the poor man felt when, one fine spring, on returning home after a shanty wintering, his wife handed him a small rickety bit of a tot, who looked like a fritter out of the frying pan, saying: "Kiss your son, my friend!"

"What is this?" exclaimed Johnny Morissette, who nearly choked himself swallowing his quid.

"This is a little angel that the good God has sent us while you were away."

"An angel! Bless my soul, my dear woman, I'd just as soon take it for a shabby attempt at a scarecrow!"

But the poor fellow had to take the brat as he was, of course—there was no help for it; and, as he seldom missed the chance of a joke, when he saw one of his chums passing his house, he would shout out:

"Hello! won't you come and have a look at my 'little angel?'"

And so the boy grew up known by all as Johnny Morissette's little angel; and with

Titange

time he came to bear no other name but that of Titange.

When I talk of his growing up, it would be a mistake to think that he ever turned out to be anything like a patch to his father. Far from it: he was born a weakling and he remained a weakling. In short, as a man, he was a dead failure.

This must have been a great worry to him, for, take my word, in the whole of my life, whether in the woods or on the rafts, I never saw such a blazing fire-brand. Although he was no bigger than my fist, as a make up, I suppose, he fussed, and fumed, and swore, and stormed like a whole shanty gang, all by himself. At every turn and mostly for no purpose, he would viciously swing his axe, and promise nothing else but to kill, to destroy, to slaughter, to rip you open and tear your heart out.

Those who knew no better took him for a demon and were scared to death; but I could size him up better than that. And then, as we were mated together, do you see, I had to bear with him such as he was. The

Christmas in French Canada

consequence was, that, in spite of his rough ways, we remained pretty good friends; and so we had a chat now and again at our work, without wasting time of course.

One morning—it was the day before Christmas—the fellow dropped his axe, and started staring at me like some one having a mighty big thing to tell.

I stopped also, and looked at him.

"Uncle Joe!" said he, spying around.

"What's up, Titange?" said I.

"Are you a safe man for a secret?"

"Did you ever hear me tattle about?"

"No, but I would like to know if I could trust you with something very particular."

"Well, that depends."

"What do you mean?"

"I mean if there is no mischief intended . . . ."

"There is no mischief whatever; the question is to go and have a little jollification to-night at old Calice Doucet's of the Banlieue?"

"Which Banlieue?"

"The Banlieue of Three Rivers, to be sure

"Every Christmas Eve there is always a nice dancing hop"

Page 228

Titange

Old Calice Doucet is a tip-top fiddler, do you see; on every Christmas Eve there is always a nice dancing hop with pretty girls at his place."

"You mean to go dancing at the Banlieue of Three Rivers to-night! More than two hundred miles through the woods, without roads or teams! Are you mad?"

"There is no need of roads or teams."

"How is that? Do you imagine you can travel as the crow flies?"

"One can travel much easier than the crow flies, uncle Joe."

"Over forests and mountains?"

"Over anything at all."

"'Pon my word, I don't understand you."

"Uncle Joe," said he, glancing once more all around as if to make sure nobody was near by; "you must have heard of the *Chasse-galerie* before this, haven't you?"

"Of course I have."

"Well?"

"Well, you don't mean to run *Chasse-galerie*, do you?"

"Why not? we are no children."

Christmas in French Canada

On my conscience and honor, my friends, on hearing that, the shivers ran down my back. I felt as if a hellish warm breath passed right in my face. I tottered on my legs, and my axe shook so in my hands that twice I missed the chalk line, a thing which had not yet happened to me that fall.

"But, Titange, my dear fellow," said I, "have you truly no fear of God?"

"Fear of God!" exclaimed the ruffian in an outburst of blasphemous laughter. "There is no God around here. Don't you know we have stored him *en cache* at the Forge village? It's all very well down below, but up the river, with all cautions taken, as long as you are all right with the Devil, everything goes."

"Will you hold your tongue, you reprobate!" said I.

"Now, now, come, uncle Joe!" said he. "Don't be such a hayseed. Here, listen to me, I'm going to tell you how the thing is worked."

And chopping ahead, he went on quietly to tell me all about the whole infernal con-

Titange

cern. A true invention of Satan himself, my friends, no more nor less. My flesh crawls only to think of it.

I must warn you, by the way, that if the town of Three Rivers has a great name for its good people, it has a mighty great one too for those who are not. And if we are to go by the set of worthless scamps it supplies every year to the lumber shanties, that reputation is not a stolen one, I tell you! I know Sorel, and I know Bytown; and I can stake my word for it, as far as roughs are concerned, there is nothing to beat Three Rivers.

If you want to know how far those scoundrels can go, listen. When they start for the shanties in the fall, they are too darn wicked to go to confession, of course; but as they still dread God somewhat, they put Him *en cache*, as they say; which means they lock Him up.

How do they go through that hellish game? This is what I am going to explain, at least according to what Titange told me.

First, they get a bottle of rum which has

Christmas in French Canada

been filled up at midnight, on All Souls' day, by the left hand of a fellow standing heels over head. This bottle they hide well in the bottom of the canoe, and they start for the St. Maurice Forges, the first station on their way up.

That's where the fine work of the devilish trick is gone through. Remember, the chapel of the village has a flight of wooden door steps. Well, when it is pitch dark, one of the scalawags lifts up one of the planks, while another empties the bottle in the hole, saying :

"*Gloria patri, gloria patro, gloria patrum.*"

To which the other replies, replacing the plank as it was :

"*Let the cat free, let the wind blow, let the boys drum !*"

"After which," added Titange, "if you are all right with old Harry, you need not fear anything for the whole winter. Beyond the Pointe-aux-Baptêmes, God is nowhere ; no saints, no angels, nothing at all ! One can work the *Chasse-galerie* every night if he wishes to. The canoe travels like wind at

"*Beyond the Pointe-aux-Baptêmes God is nowhere*"

Titange

hundreds of feet above the earth; and as long as you do not utter the name of Christ, or of the Virgin, and you take care not to run against the church steeples, you can paddle thousands of miles almost in the twinkling of an eye. Isn't that smart?"

"And this is what you are after tonight?" said I.

"Yes," he replied.

"And you want to take me along with you?"

"That's it. We are five already; if you join us, it will make six: just one at the bow, another at the helm, and two paddlers on each side. I have thought of you, uncle Joe, because of your brawny arm, of your sharp sight and your spunk. Now, say yes, and we shall have a high old time to-night."

"What! and this on the holy Christmas Eve, too . . . ! Do you think of it?" said I.

"Why, this is nothing but fun, and Christmas is a day of rejoicings, you know that."

As you may well think, my friends, although Fiddle Joe may not be a Christian of

Christmas in French Canada

the first water, I couldn't stand such profanity without being startled. But at the same time I must declare that I had often heard of this invention of Satan called *Chasse-galerie;* I had even seen it, as I have already said, in broad daylight, right in front of the church of St. Jean Deschaillons; and I shall not deny that I was rather anxious to know how those scamps managed the infernal machine. In fact, my friends, to tell you the whole truth, I had a kind of notion to witness the thing with my own eyes.

"Well, what have you to say to this, uncle Joe?" said Titange, "are you in it?"

"*Ma frime!* old fellow," said I, "I don't say no. Are you sure there is no danger?"

"Not the slightest. I'll go bail for that."

"Well, I think I'll chime in."

"Well done! I may depend upon you?"

"Honest! When shall we start?"

"As soon as the boss is asleep; at half-past nine, the latest."

"Where?"

"You know where the big drive canoe lies?"

Titange

" Yes."

" That's the one we'll take; don't fail to be there in time. In less than half an hour we'll be at old Doucet's. And then, hurrah, boys, with the 'double-double,' the *gigue simple*, and the 'pigeon-wings.' You'll see, uncle Joe, how we twist up a midnight mass, we boys of Three Rivers!"

And so saying the rash fellow started a quickstep on his piece of timber, clogging his heels as if he had been already hopping at old Calice Doucet's, with the girls of the Banlieue of Three Rivers.

As for me, my friends, I was far from feeling so merry. In fact, I was more than ill at ease, I was dreadfully scared; but I had my plan, of course.

So, I wasn't late on the spot. At half-past nine sharp, and before the others had turned out, I had time to pin a small picture of the Infant Jesus right on the stem of the craft.

"There!" said I to myself, "this is stronger than all the evil spirits of damnation: we shall see what's going to happen."

Christmas in French Canada

"All aboard, all aboard, quick!" whispered Titange, falling in with four other worthless chaps, and taking his place at the stern. "Uncle Joe, you have keen eyes, sit in front. The others at the paddles! No scapulars on any of you?"

"No."

"No medals?"

"No."

"Nothing holy, you understand?"

"No."

"All right, then. You are ready! Attention now . . ! Let every one repeat after me:

> *Satan, our master fair,*
> *Heave us up in the air . . .*
> *Wing, wang, wong!*
> *Wong, wang, wing!*
> *Drive us along*
> *On the night's dark wing! . . .*

Now paddle on! paddle on, boys! . . . Damn it, paddle on! . . . ."

But it was no go, my friends. Vainly did Titange and his comrades paddle as if to save their lives, the canoe didn't stir.

Titange

"How is this?" shouted out Titange, with a dreadful oath. "You did not repeat correct after me; let us begin over again!"

We began over again, but it was no use; the craft remained motionless in the snow, like a dead trunk.

"By damnation!" cried Titange with a string of oaths; "some of you are cheating. Step out, one after the other, we shall see who is the confounded traitor."

We stepped out one after the other as he said; but for no good; the machine did not move an inch.

"By all thunders!" swore out the little man, "I shall go alone; and may all the devils of the St. Maurice hang the whole set of you by the neck . . . *Satan, our master fair . . . .*"

And the reprobate went on with the devilish imprecation.

But, far from travelling "on the night's dark wing," Titange couldn't jump over a fence, and we didn't see even the wing of a bat.

The canoe was frozen dead.

Christmas in French Canada

Then, my friends, it was a tempest the sole remembrance of which makes my hair stand on end.

"My axe! my axe! where is my axe?" yelled the ranter; "I'll kill! I'll murder! I'll massacre! . . . My axe, I tell you!"

Bad luck! there was one at the bottom of the canoe. He grabbed the tool, and standing up straight on one of the crossings, wild with rage, he swung it three or four times around his head like a desperate maniac.

It was terrible; but at the same time it was a real curiosity, my friends, to see this insignificant little bit of a man who looked like a consumptive mosquito, raising such an infernal row. A pack of mad hounds couldn't have been more noisy.

The whole shanty flocked out, of course, and witnessed the dreadful scene.

Titange had it in for the canoe now:

"You accursed rascal," he cried, "I have said all the words correct: you must start, or I'll know the reason why."

And saying so, he darted forth with his

Titange

axe, to demolish the bow of the craft, where my little picture stood fast on the stem.

Goodness of my soul! we had time only to utter a cry. The axe, catching in a branch, had whirled out of his hand, and fallen back right on the outstretched arm of the miscreant, whom the shock had hurled headlong to the bottom of the canoe.

The sinews of his wrist were clean cut . . .

At twelve o'clock that night, the whole shanty, moved by the terrible ordeal, knelt down for once, and fervently offered an honest prayer to the newly born Redeemer.

On New Year, an old missionary visited our camp, and we, as one man, confessed our sins—Titange first of all.

Full of repentance, and confused for having so poorly succeeded in putting *le bon Dieu en cache*, he moreover took advantage of the good priest's company to make his way down to Three Rivers, without thinking for a moment, I'll stake my word for it, of sparking with the girls at old Calice Doucet's of the Banlieue.

Christmas in French Canada

Some two years later, happening to stop at the St. Maurice Forges, I saw, on the steps of the chapel, a poor ailing beggar holding out a hand with fingers crooked, distorted and twisted like a Christmas *croquignole*.

I drew near to give him a penny: it was my former timber mate, old Johnny Morissette's little angel: Titange!

And *cric, crac!* . . . Et cetera.

The Loup Garou.

"HAVE you heard that *la belle Mérance à Glaude Couture** is going to be married?"

"No."

"Well, she is; the

---

* The present story is not wholly original, some of its features being traditional among our peasants under more or less different forms. The *loup-garou* is nothing else than the wehrwolf of the German legend founded on the belief that some people could trans-

Christmas in French Canada

banns are to be published next week."

"Married to whom?"

"Guess."

"It's pretty hard to guess: *la belle Mérance* is surrounded with sweethearts by the score every Sunday that God brings along."

"With Baptiste Octeau, I bet!"

"No."

"It must be to Damase Lapointe, then."

"Not at all... *Ma foi*, it's just as well to tell you at once: she is going to be married to Captain Gosselin, of St. Nicolas."

"To Captain Gosselin, of St. Nicolas?"

"Exactly."

"Well I declare!"

"You don't say so!"

"She is to take such a miscreant?"

"Well, the fellow is well off, you know;

---

form themselves into wolves at pleasure. In French Canada, though, a moral has been added to the fantastic tradition: the *loup-garou*, here, is not a sorcerer, but a victim of irreligion. A man who has been seven years without partaking of the Easter Sacrament falls a prey to the infernal power, and may be condemned to rove about every night in the shape and skin of a wolf, or any other kind of animal, according to the nature of his sins. A bloody wound only can release him.

The Loup-Garou

He has made her a present of a nice gold brooch and a diamond ring, and Mérance doesn't sneer at that, I tell you."

"Any how! I wouldn't marry him, even though he were a *seigneur*, and owned all the farms of the parish."

"Neither I: a man who has no religion.."

"Who has not fulfilled his Easter duties for years..."

"Who never goes to church..."

"Nor to confession..."

"Who is going to be bewitched into some horrible *loup-garou* some day."

"It's doomed fate for him, if he passes seven years without absolution for his sins."

"Poor Mérance, it's too bad!.."

"'Tis no fun to have your husband converted every evening into a beast roaming wildly along the roads, through the woods, God knows where. I would just as soon marry old Harry himself."

"It is true that there would be a means of releasing him."

"How?"

"By wounding him, of course; by pricking

Christmas in French Canada

his forehead, by cutting his ear, his nose, his tail, anything at all, with some sharp instrument, the main thing being to draw blood."

"And the beast will be again a man?"

"At once."

"Why, thanks! As for me, I prefer a man that needs not to be bled."

"So do I," exclaimed all the girls.

"You believe in such silly tales!" cried a voice: "you set of fools!"

The foregoing conversation was held at an old farmer's of St. Antoine de Tilly, where a number of young people from the neighborhood had gathered for an *épluchette de blé-d'Inde*—corn bee—which was to be followed by a griddle cake *réveillon*.

As can be seen, the company was indulging in a general chat; and from one subject to the other, the *loup-garou* legend had fallen on the tapis.

Of course it is useless to add that the scene takes us back to a great many years ago, for—fortunately—our country folk give but very little attention now to these queer superstitions of the past.

The Loup-Garou

The interruption brought out by the last speaker is, besides, an evidence that, even in those days, and among our illiterate people, these mysterious traditions found some unbelievers.

"All these are grandmother's stories!" added the same voice in answer to the almost unanimous protest to which the irreverent sally had given rise.

"Tut, tut, tut!.. It is not well to treat one's own grandmother with contempt, my young fellow!" intervened an old woman, who, taking no part in the *épluchette*, pursued silently her knitting at the light of the hearth, which threw fitful and intermittent glimmers on her long wrinkled face.

"Old people know more than the young," added she; "and when you have trod my path, you'll not be so ready to scoff at those who believe in the old stories."

"So you believe in *loup-garous*, mother Catherine?" said the young interrupter with a provoking smile.

"Had you known Joachim Crête as I

Christmas in French Canada

have, you could not but believe in them also, my friend," retorted the old woman.

"I have already heard of that story of Joachim Crête," said one of the hearers; "why shouldn't you tell it, mother Catherine?"

I have no objection, said she, dipping her thumb and fore-finger into an old horn snuff-box. It does not harm young folks to know what may happen to those who have no respect for religion and sneer at things they do not understand. It's an old saying with me that the fear of God is never out of place.

Unfortunately, poor Joachim Crête didn't think so.

He was not precisely what may be called a wicked man, oh no! but he was like many others of our own time: he thought of God and performed his duties only when he had nothing else to do. This is not what helps a man ahead, my friends.

He wouldn't have cheated a neighbor out of a copper, no doubt; he observed Lent and Fridays as well as anyone, they said. But he

The Loup-Garou

partook of the holy sacraments at Easter-time only—once a year and no more; he winked jeeringly when somebody spoke of the church collections; and besides, without being a regu-

"*Joachim Crête was proprietor of a mill.*"

lar drunkard, he was fond enough of the drop to go to bed, every Saturday night, too fuddled to mind if his mill was running on Sunday.

For I must tell you, my friends, that

Christmas in French Canada

Joachim Crête was proprietor of a mill, a corn mill, situated in the *concession* of Beauséjour, on the little river called La Rigole.

Of course it wasn't anything like a seigneurial mill, but it worked the best it could, and ground its oats and corn, any way. I fancy I can see it yet, the old mill, seated right alongside the *chemin du roi*. When we used to go to catechism for our first communion, we little folk never failed to stop there for a rest.

There it was that I got acquainted with the wretched man—a man about forty, who had no objection to tease little girls, I may add without any mischievous meaning.

As he was unmarried, he had fixed up a small dwelling inside the mill, where he lived like a bear with a hired man by the name of Hubert Sauvageau, a fellow who had travelled in the *pays d'en haut*, who had lived on the rafts, who had been knocking about for years, without—it was evident—having learned much for the benefit of his soul.

How had he come to settle at St. Antoine

The Loup-Garou

after such wanderings? Nobody ever knew, All I can say is that if Joachim Crête was not exactly a model for the parish, it was not his hired man who could give him lessons on principles, as people say.

With all deference to the company, the fellow had no more religion than a dog. Never was he seen at church; never did he take off his hat to the Calvary; he hardly saluted the *curé* with the end of his fingers when he met him on the road. In fact, he was a man of poor reputation indeed.

"What's all this to me?" said Joachim Crête when the matter was referred to in his presence; "he is a quiet fellow who never faints at work; he is reliable, just as sober as myself; he eats no more than another, and plays checkers to put in the time with me: nobody would give me better satisfaction, even though he wore out his knees, from morning till night, at *le chemin de la Croix.*"

As you see by his own words, Joachim Crête was a checker player. And a good one too, for if anybody had ever won a

Christmas in French Canada

game of *polonaise* against him no one in all St. Antoine could boast of having seen him lose more than a *partie simple*.

But one must suppose that the fellow Sauvageau was a pretty good match for him, as—especially when the miller had returned home from town in the course of the day with a demijohn—those who passed by the mill in the evening heard them yell, each one in his turn: "*Mange! Soufflé! Franc-coin! Partie nulle!*" And so forth, as in a rage of ambition.

But let me reach the adventure you wish me to relate.

On that day—it was Christmas Eve—and Joachim Crête had returned from Quebec rather tipsy, and — useless to add—with a fine stock of supplies in the box of his cariole for the festivities.

The whole mill was in merriment.

My grand uncle, old José Corriveau, who had a bagful of grain to mill, called in the evening and said to Joachim Crête:

"You are going to attend midnight mass, of course?"

The Loup-Garou

A grin was the only answer. It was Hubert Sauvageau coming in, and seating himself in a corner with his pipe.

"We shall see about that," he said.

"No joke, young men!" added old Corriveau, walking out; "the midnight mass is not a thing to be missed."

And he left, with his whip in his hand.

"Ha! ha! ha! . . ." laughed Sauvageau; "but we shall first play a game of checkers, won't we, monsieur Joachim?"

"Ten if you wish, old fellow; but before all, we must have a smile," was the reply.

And the spree had commenced

At about eleven o'clock, a neighbor by the name of Vincent Dubé knocked at the door:

"Look here, Joachim," said he, "if you want a place in my *berlot* to go to the midnight mass, there is one for you, as I am alone with the old woman."

"Thank you, I've got my own horse," answered Joachim Crête.

"Are they going to bother us much longer with their midnight mass?" grumbled Hubert Sauvageau when the door was closed.

Christmas in French Canada

"Let us have a drink," said the miller.

And hurrah with the glasses and the checkers!

The people who passed by, going to church, riding or on foot, said to each other:

"Why, Joachim Crête's mill is still running; he must have quantities to grind."

"Surely he won't go on working on Christmas, will he?"

"I wouldn't be surprised."

"Especially if his accursed Sauvageau has a hand in it..."

And so on. In the meanwhile, the mill went on rolling, the game of checkers didn't stop, and the drinking continued. Toasts were endless.

Some one knocked at the window:

"Hold on, you fellows; it's near twelve. The last bell is pealing. It's not very Christian-like, what you are doing there."

Two voices answered:

"Go to blazes! Let us have peace!"

The last passers-by vanished. And the mill went on rolling. As the weather was

"*Look here Joachim, if you want a place in my berlot, there is one for you*"

The Loup-Garou

calm and quiet, its rumbling noise was heard afar, and the good people hurried away, making the sign of the Cross on their breast.

Although the church was nearly two miles distant from the mill Joachim Crête could hear clearly the sound of the bell. At the last toll he felt a kind of remorse:

"'Tis twelve," said he; "if we raised the paddle-door. . ."

"Pshaw! are you such a poltroon?" said Sauvageau. "Here! let us have a horn, and then I'll make you capot."

"Ah! well, as to that, you are not fit for it, my young man. . . Help yourself, and here's your luck!"

"Here's yours, monsieur Joachim."

They had barely replaced their tumblers on the table, when the last sound of the bell passed over the mill like a whisper in the wind.

It was as rapid as thought. . . Crac!. . the mill was stopped dead, just as if a thunderbolt had broken the machinery. A deep silence followed, through which one could have heard the creeping of a mouse.

Christmas in French Canada

"What's the matter?" cried out Joachim Crête.

"Some impudent jokers, no doubt," said the hired man.

"Let us go and see, quick!"

A lantern was lit, and our two checker players started with uncertain step in the direction of the undershot-wheel. But vainly did they search and poke everywhere; all was in good order, nothing seemed to have been interfered with.

"This is most extraordinary," they said, quite nonplussed.

At all events, they oiled the machine, started her again, and returned to their checker-board — not without making their first call at the table, though.

"Your health, Hubert."

"This is to yours, monsieur Joachim."

But hardly were the glasses emptied, when the two men started staring at each other with a bewildered expression: they were beastly drunk first of all, and then the mill had become silent once more.

"Some confounded rascals have thrown

The Loup-Garou

rubbish into the grindstones," muttered Joachim Crête.

"Let the devil wring my neck," jabbered Sauvageau, "if we don't find what's wrong this time."

And here are once more our two drunkards, lantern in hand, prowling everywhere about the mill, stumbling and tripping on everything they came across.

But all uselessly; there was nothing the matter either in the grindstones or elsewhere.

The machine was started again, but *ouichte!* half a turn of the wheel, and that was all. The whole mechanism was at a dead stand still.

"The Devil take the whole concern!" yelled out Joachim Crête; "let us go!"

A desperate oath was uttered. Hubert Sauvageau, who had probably entangled his feet in some kind of obstacle, had fallen headlong on the floor like a helpless brute.

The lantern had gone out of his hand, to be sure; so that it was pitch dark, and Joachim Crête, who had all he could do to

Christmas in French Canada

steer himself, had no great mind to go to the rescue of his companion.

"Let the rogue look after himself as best he can!" said he; "I'm going for a drink."

And by the dim light of the candle which glimmered in the distance through the half-opened door, he succeeded, after many stumbles and slips, to worm his way into the room, where he entered without closing the door behind him, so as to give the loiterer a chance to do the same.

As soon as he had passed the threshold, you may well imagine that his first thought was to go right to the table where the glasses and bottles stood; but as he was pouring out a gobletful of rum, swinging on his hips, he heard behind his back something like a groan.

"That's you?" he said without turning; "here you are, come on!"

Another moaning answered, stronger than the first.

"What's the matter? .. Did you hurt yourself? .. Have a drink, that'll cure you."

But no one appeared nor responded.

Quite surprised, Joachim Crête turned

The Loup-Garou

around, laying his glass on the table, and stood terrified, with eyes fearfully fixed and his hair standing on end.

It wasn't at all Hubert Sauvageau who was facing him; it was a huge black dog, as tall as a man, with formidable teeth, sitting on his haunches, and who stared at him with eyes blazing like embers.

Without being a hero, the miller was not precisely a coward: after his first impression of terror, he plucked up courage and called out to Hubert.

"Who has let this dog in?"

No answer.

"Hubert!" he insisted, stammering with a thick voice; "where does this dog come from?"

Not a word.

"Why, that's rather cool. . . Get out of this, you!"

The big dog gave a growl that sounded like a bit of laughter, but didn't stir a foot.

And Hubert was nowhere to be seen.

Joachim was anything but merry, as you may reckon. He couldn't understand what

Christmas in French Canada

was going on; and as a dreadful fright was creeping over him again, he thought of making for the door. But the terrible dog had only to turn his head with his blazing eyes to bar the way. Seeing this, the poor man crawled backwards to take refuge between the table and the bed, without losing sight of the monster.

"*And he fell on his knees.*"

The latter advanced a few steps with another hellish growl.

"Hubert!" cried out the unfortunate man in a tone of horrible anguish.

The dog kept moving towards him, erect

The Loup-Garou

on his legs, growling more and more, and keeping his burning eyes fastened on the trembling man.

"Help! help! . ." howled Joachim Crête, crazy with fear, and backing himself up to the wall.

None answered his call, but at that very moment the church bell pealing for the Elevation was heard.

Then a thought of repentance passed through the brains of the wretched man.

"It is a loup-garou!" cried he; "my God, forgive me!"

And he fell on his knees.

At the same time the infernal beast darted upon him.

Fortunately the poor miller, while kneeling down, had felt something on the wall that caught him by the clothes.

It was a reaping-hook.

The man instinctively seized the weapon and hit the brute right on the head.

It was the matter of one instant. Everything disappeared in the dark. In the struggle, short as it had been, the table had been over-

Christmas in French Canada

turned, and the glasses, bottles and candle were scattered on the floor.

As to Joachim Crête, he had fainted away.

When he returned to his senses, somebody was throwing cold water in his face, and a well-known voice was saying:

"What has been the matter with you, monsieur Joachim?"

"Is that you, Hubert?"

"As you see."

"Where is he?"

"Whom do you mean?"

"The dog."

"Which dog?"

"The *loup-garou*."

"What?"

"The *loup-garou* I have released with my reaping-hook."

"Good Heavens! have you gone mad, Monsieur Joachim?"

"I have not dreamt that surely... And yourself, where are you from?"

"From the mill."

"I see it is running now, the mill..."

"You can hear it."

The Loup-Garou

"Go and stop it right off; it must not work on Christmas."

"Why, Christmas is passed, it was yesterday."

"How is that?"

"You have been senseless for two days, that's all."

"Is it possible? . . But what is the matter with your ear? . . Blood!"

"That's nothing."

"How did you get that? Speak out!"

"Don't you remember I had a fall in the mill on Christmas Eve?"

"Yes."

"Well, I cut my ear on the edge of a pail."

Joachim Crête, my friends, sat up on his bed, haggard and shaken by a shiver of horror. . .

"Ah! damnable wretch!" cried he; "it was you! . . "

And the poor fellow fell back on his pillow, never to recover his wits again.

He died ten years later in a lunatic asylum.

Christmas in French Canada

As to the mill, it was torn down and carried away in the spring, at the breaking up of the ice.

. . . .

"Césaire!" whispered a sweet voice in the ear of the young man whose incredulity had provoked old Catherine's story; "a red head of corn!"

"Is that so? . . Give!" said he stealthily.

And rising on his feet:

"My friends," added he with a joyful exclamation, "a red head of corn! . . I claim my rights!" *

And, to the applause of all, the young man bowed to his right, and impressed a loving kiss on the blushing cheek of his fair neighbor.

"And so help me God," said he, "that's all the sorcery I believe in!"

---

* In an *épluchette de blé-d' Inde*, whoever finds a red head of corn has a right to kiss the young girl of his choice.

www.ingramcontent.com/pod-product-compliance
Lightning Source LLC
Chambersburg PA
CBHW030739230426
43667CB00007B/779